The
Medical Mind
of
Shakespeare

Ex Libris

~~~~~

_____

_____

_____

And Aesculapius guide us*
Pericles, Prince of Tyre, III, ii, 118

---

*Coronis, the mother of the unborn Aesculapius by Apollo, was killed by
Artemis for unfaithfulness. Her body was about to be buried on the pyre,
when Apollo snatched the boy from his mother's womb and from the
flames and carried him to the cave of the wise Centaur Chiron, who
instructed him in the cure of all diseases. Aesculapius thus became the
great god of medicine to the Greeks. He is generally depicted as carrying
a staff with a serpent entwined upon it. The serpent was an ancient
symbol of health, because it could shed its skin and appear young again.

THE
MEDICAL MIND
OF
SHAKESPEARE

AUBREY C. KAIL,
M.B., B.S., M.R.C.P. (Edin.)

WILLIAMS & WILKINS
ADIS PTY LIMITED

DESIGNED BY ROBIN JAMES

First published in 1986 by
Williams & Wilkins • ADIS Pty Limited
404 Sydney Road (PO Box 132) Balgowlah NSW 2093
Copyright © Williams & Wilkins • ADIS Pty Limited

National Library of Australia
Cataloguing in publication data
Kail, Aubrey C.
The medical mind of Shakespeare.
Includes index.
ISBN 0 86433 013 8.
1. Shakespeare, William, 1564-1616 — Knowledge —
Medicine, I. Title.
822.3'3

Typeset in 14/16 Cloister with Cloister Open Face
by Adtype Photocomposition Pty. Ltd.
Printed in Hong Kong by Leefung Asco Printers Ltd

In a work such as this it is not always possible to
acknowledge, or even find, the copyright holder of certain
material. The publishers have made every effort, but apologise
in advance for any lapse. They would be pleased to hear
from anyone who has not been acknowledged.

Portions of this book were published in
The Medical Journal of Australia between October and December,
1983, and are reprinted here with permission.

CONTENTS

AUTHOR'S NOTE

HE NUMBERING OF ACTS, scenes and lines follows that of the well-known Alexander text of William Shakespeare (1978). Various texts and papers to which passing reference is made, or which in some way have contributed to the understanding of the work, are listed in the bibliography.

My thanks are due to Mrs Alison Holster, former Librarian of The Royal Australasian College of Physicians. Without the assistance of Mrs Holster this book would probably have bogged down early in its preparation. Miss Dorothy Tremlett provided much needed expertise with the reading of the manuscript. Mr Bob Thomas of Canberra, and his wife, Connie Thomas, were also very helpful with constructive criticism of the manuscript. To them and to Mrs Margaret Tipka, my patient and efficient secretary, my thanks are due. A special word of acknowledgement is tendered to my wife and daughters, without whose continued support the work would never have eventuated. Finally, I would like to thank Pamela Petty, of Williams & Wilkins – Adis Pty Limited, for many suggestions and assistance in many ways.

FOREWORD

ROBABLY NO LITERARY CORPUS, other than the Bible and the Talmud, has endured as many post-mortem examinations as the works of William Shakespeare. Certainly few have been examined from so many disparate professional aspects; Shakespeare has been studied specifically from the viewpoints of the lawyer, the doctor, the classical mythologist, the religionist, the historian, the political scientist and the botanist, not to mention as an angler, archer and apothecary. Medical commentary began essentially with *The Medical Knowledge of Shakespeare* (London, 1860) by Sir John Bucknill, an eminent and innovative British psychiatrist. Bucknill, in his fulsome dedication to Lord Campbell, then Lord High Chancellor of England, acknowledged that his book owed its origin 'in great measure' to Campbell's *Shakespeare's Legal Requirements* (London, 1859), which, in effect, argued that Shakespeare's legal knowledge was so extensive and detailed that he must have had legal training. Bucknill showed that Shakespeare's appreciation of ancient and contemporary medicine was at least equally as profound, but he disavowed 'the intention to put forward on behalf of his own profession any rival claims'.

Bucknill's circumspection has been justified by the judgement of time, which allows an educated gentleman of the period a wide range of expertise, or at least of understanding. His delicately implied criticism of Lord Campbell is more bluntly stated by a later commentator,* who observed that the Lord Chancellor 'was more famed for his brilliancy than for his accuracy'. Nonetheless, Shakespeare's legal and medical learning, amongst other expressions of his universal genius, was added to an alleged allegorical and political interpretation of the plays to 'prove' that Francis Bacon, a lawyer and philosopher of science, was the real author. It is a coincidence that these views should be most strongly espoused by a doctor, William Thomson, who was a Scottish graduate and a migrant to Australia; Dr Aubrey C. Kail holds a Scottish postgraduate diploma and is also a migrant to this country. Thomson's major, but by no means his only, publication on the Baconian theme was *On Renascence Drama, or History Made Visible* (Melbourne, 1880). But in the direct line of medical commentary, other than innumerable journal articles, the next work of any significance is R. R. Simpson's *Shakespeare and Medicine* (Edinburgh, 1959); his book owes much to Bucknill, but brings many of the technical and scientific interpretations up to date.

Why, then, should we welcome Dr Kail's further contribution to what may seem a well-born theme? The answer is

---

*J. M. Beck, foreword to *Links between Shakespeare and the Law,* by D. B. Barton, London, 1928.

---

simple: Dr Kail presents Shakespeare's medical knowledge for the joy of it, reflecting the delight he has had as an enthusiastic Shakespearian in recognising references to his professional interest and appreciating their significance. He has the common touch, for he dwells mostly on interesting or important references which might be obscure to the layman, or to someone unfamiliar with ancient or Elizabethan medicine. He provides an appropriate, if occasionally simplified, background of historical and technical information. His survey reveals a light and sometimes humorous touch, drawing upon many allusions which are not necessarily medical, at least in the technical sense. Bucknill and Simpson may not be ignored by the academic, but Dr Kail has succeeded in producing a delightfully readable book for Everyman, or at least for every man (or woman; such literary style as I possess recoils against spoiling the word play by writing 'person') who derives enjoyment from reading or watching Shakespeare's plays. To some extent, his less studious approach reflects the likely or anticipated reactions of the audience of Shakespeare's day; health and disease are the concern of all levels of society in every age, as many another dramatist, including Shakespeare's contemporaries, has appreciated. If there is a difference in Shakespeare's use of medical allusion by comparison with Marlowe, Jonson, Webster and Ford, Beaumont and Fletcher, and the rest of those prolific and ingenious dramatists, it lies in his use of it in imagery and in the subtle creation of atmosphere, rather than simply as a relevant or peripheral element in the narrative. But this is another matter, although one which the reader may care to consider for himself as he reviews Dr Kail's quotations and their contexts.

My qualifications for writing this introduction can be no more than an interest in the history of medicine and an isolated and undistinguished paper on medical allusion in one of Shakespeare's plays published some thirty years ago. I am thus particularly honoured to introduce a book which must enjoy a wide and appreciative audience.

BRYAN GANDEVIA, A.M., M.D., F.R.A.C.P.
Associate Professor of Medicine and Chairman of
the Department of Respiratory Medicine,
The Prince Henry and Prince of Wales Hospitals, Sydney.

INTRODUCTION

OR OVER 300 YEARS, people have responded to Shakespeare's plays and speculated about the man who wrote them. Today the names of some of his characters – Hamlet, Macbeth, Romeo, Juliet, Lear – are household names, familiar to people who have never read his plays or even seen them acted. Many of his lines have become part of everyday language, and his philosophy, poetry and artistry have been the subject of universal study and praise.

It is amazing how much light Shakespeare's plays throw on the social history of his time. Even more interesting to some of us are his references to medical and scientific matters. In thirty-seven plays he mentions practically all the diseases and drugs that were known in those days. In one single scene in *Troilus and Cressida* (Act V, Scene i) there is a long list of diseases that the flesh was heir to in his day: 'Now, the rotten diseases of the south [regarded as an unhealthy region], the guts-griping, ruptures, catarrhs, loads o' gravel i' the back, lethargies, cold palsies, raw eyes, dirt-rotten livers, wheezing lungs, bladders full of imposthume [abscess], sciaticas, limekilns i' th' palm [arthritis], incurable bone-ache, and the rivelled fee-simple [permanent ownership] of the tetter [eruption]'. In the same scene we find mentioned 'sore eye', 'gall', 'ear-wax', 'too much blood and too little brain', 'lazar' [leper], and 'incontinent varlets'.

Shakespeare's plays bear witness to a profound knowedge of contemporary physiology and psychology, and he employed medical terms in a manner which would have been beyond the powers of any ordinary playwright or physician.

Shakespeare justified the custom of medical note-taking (*Macbeth*, V, i, 31). His plays revealed many current medical doctrines, including the doctrine of the humours – the belief that our bodies consist of the four elements, fire, air, earth and water. He dwelt on the therapeutic value of herbs and plants, and on the old beliefs of the influences of the planets on disease and of the moon on the mind. Even the quackery of his age was given its fair share of notice. He was well acquainted with the wasteful practice of blood-letting, which was frequently performed in those days. Shakespeare had a working knowledge of many organs and structures of the body, of air and climate, of syphilis, obstetrics and public health, of mental disorders and surgery; this will be illustrated by many quotations. He exhibited the feelings associated with the tragedy of suffering and the influence of sympathy upon the patient, the relationship between hope and prognosis, the value of mirth, the evils of alcohol, the pangs of insomnia and the benefits of sleep and, finally, the attributes of death. This book is an attempt to put some of this together in a manner which may interest the medical as well as the non-medical reader.

To
Sylvia
Alison, Shelley

Ellen Terry as Lady Macbeth (*Macbeth*, Act V, Scene I); from *The Complete Works of William Shakespeare* (c. 1910). Photograph: Window & Grove, London.

1
SHAKESPEARE'S
PHYSICIANS

Give physic to the sick, ease to the pained.
The Rape of Lucrece, 901

HAKESPEARE'S SON-IN-LAW, Dr John Hall, was a physician. Susanna Shakespeare, his eldest daughter, in 1607 married John Hall, who was only seven years younger than her father. He was the son of a medical practitioner Dr William Hall, of Acton in Middlesex, and was a graduate of Queen's College, Cambridge. Like many others, he undertook further studies in Europe, and after returning to England, settled in Stratford-on-Avon in 1600, in the fine house which is now known as Hall's Croft and is open to the public. He married Susanna seven years later. Hall died in 1635 at the age of 60, and his gravestone is second to the right of Shakespeare's in Holy Trinity Church, Stratford.

In his 35 years at Stratford, Hall built up a large and far-flung practice. About a year after Shakespeare's death, in 1616, Hall began to write up records of various patients whom he had attended and the results of his treatment. He recorded about 1000 cases, and his original notes are preserved in the British Museum. Curiously, he wrote in an abbreviated form of Latin which was difficult to decipher, but his notes were edited and put into English by Dr James Cooke of Warwick, who described himself as 'a Practitioner of

[17]

Physick and Chirurgery'. They were published in 1657 under the title 'Select Observations on English Bodies or Cures both Empirical and Historical, performed on very Eminent Persons in Desperate Diseases'. Many of his distinguished patients were sufferers from scurvy, for which no adequate treatment existed at that time. Dr Cooke's book proved very popular and was reprinted twice.

In 1626, Charles I, at the time of his coronation, resorted to a unique and royal technique of raising funds by selling knighthoods. A knighthood was offered to Dr John Hall, who declined the honour, but nevertheless paid the King the sum of £10 for the offer. Hall's death, in 1635, is recorded in the Register as: '1635, Nov 26, B. Johannes Hall, medicus pertissimus'. His tombstone in the chancel of the parish church of Stratford bears his coat-of-arms, and the first lines of his inscription read: 'Hallius hic situs est medica celeberrimus arte'. 'Medicus pertissimus' and 'medica celeberrimus' were high praise for any man, even in terms of tombstone eulogies, and reflected the esteem in which this successful and popular medical practitioner was held by the local community.

It seems quite possible that John Hall provided his father-in-law with a fair amount of medical information or technical knowledge. By 1600, the year in which Hall arrived in Stratford, Shakespeare had already written about 20 plays, and the remainder were written between 1600 and 1613. Thus, he may or may not have benefited from the medical knowledge of his son-in-law. Medical references abound in some plays; for example, there are a great number in 2 *King Henry IV*, Act I, Scene ii, and this play was written in 1597-1598, before Dr John Hall arrived in Stratford.

Arms of the College of Physicians on Royal
Charter, 1546; reproduced by permission of the
Registrar of the Royal College of Physicians.

Shakespeare's medical references are explicit, they occur frequently, and in many instances they show a quite extraordinary depth of understanding. However, the same observation applies to his references to nature, music, philosophy, and all sorts of other subjects. They were all products of his unique mind.

Shakespeare introduced eight medical characters into seven of his plays; they were:

Doctor Caius, a French physician, in *The Merry Wives of Windsor*.

A doctor in *King Lear*.

An English doctor in *Macbeth*.

A Scots doctor in *Macbeth*.

Cornelius, a physician, in *Cymbeline*.

Cerimon, a lord of Ephesus, and also a physician, in *Pericles, Prince of Tyre*.

Dr Butts, physician to the King, in *King Henry VIII*.

Gerard de Narbon in *All's Well That Ends Well*, who although dead, was represented by his clever daughter Helena.

Only four of the eight physicians were named – Caius, Cornelius, Cerimon and Butts. The others were kept anonymous. There are neither surgeons nor apothecaries in his plays, although these are referred to frequently by other characters.

Strangely, the one doctor whom Shakespeare holds up to ridicule is Dr Caius, who was the first to appear *(Merry Wives of Windsor)*. He was presented as rather a strange man, a Frenchman, with insufficient knowledge of English, and was made the butt of many jokes in that merry play. The Dr Caius of Shakespeare is made comic by his French accent and his strange behaviour. He challenges Evans, a Welshman, to a duel over a girl, and the whole adventure turns into a flop. His namesake was Dr John Caius,* founder of Caius College, Cambridge, who was physician to Edward VI, Queen Mary and Queen Elizabeth, just as Dr Caius in the play was Court Physician to Windsor. He is considered an eccentric by his companions, and at the scene of the duel is told by Sir Hugh Evans, a Welsh parson *(Merry Wives of Windsor,* III, i, 77):

> *Evans. [Aside to Caius]* Pray you, let us not be laughing-stocks to other men's humours; I desire you in friendship, and I will one way or other make you amends. *[Aloud]* I will knog your urinals† about your knave's cogscomb for missing your meetings and appointments.

Dr Caius was treated more as a figure of fun than as a regular physician, and it was probable that Shakespeare meant to represent a quack and not the real and learned Dr Caius. A knowledge of Galen and Hippocrates was the standard by which a physician was judged, and Hugh Evans, the Welsh parson, expresses his opinion of poor Dr Caius *(Merry Wives of Windsor,* III, i, 60):

> *Evans.* He has no more knowledge in Hibocrates and Galen, and he is a knave besides.

---

*Dr John Caius (1510-1573), a scholar and linguist, followed the ideals of Linacre, who founded the Royal College of Physicians, and upon whom he is said to have modelled himself. Like all his contemporaries, he did not doubt the validity of the humoral hypothesis in the cause of disease. He was elected President of the Royal College of Physicians nine times.
†urinals: a doctor's glass for testing urine by inspection.

The physician in *King Lear* makes a brief appearance and has the traditional role of a physician-philosopher. He is questioned by Lear's youngest daughter, Cordelia, concerning her father's progressive breakdown and mental illness. He is a resourceful man, and his treatment of the old King is humane and wise. This is remarkable, for the treatment of insanity at that time and long afterwards was, as Rosalind put it in *As You Like It* (III, ii, 270), 'a dark house and a whip'. He has interesting comments to make on the deteriorating mental state of Lear (*Lear*, IV, iv, 8):

> *Cordelia*...What can man's wisdom,
> In.the restoring his bereaved sense?
> He that helps him, take all my outward worth.[1]
> *Doctor*. There is means, madam.
> Our foster-nurse of nature is repose,
> The which he lacks; that to provoke in him
> Are many simples operative,[2] whose power
> Will close the eye of anguish.

He advocates rest ('repose'), and expects improvement when the King is awakened from his sleep by the sound of music (*Lear*, IV, vii, 15):

> *Cordelia*. Cure this great breach in his abused nature!
> Th' untun'd and jarring senses, O, wind up
> Of this child-changed[3] father!
> *Doctor*.   So please your Majesty
> That we may wake the King; he hath slept long.
> *Cordelia* Be govern'd by your knowledge, and proceed
> I' th' sway' of your own will.
> ...

Doctor. Be by, good madam, when we do awake him;
I doubt not of his temperance.[5]

...

Doctor. Be comforted, good madam. The great rage,
You see, is kill'd in him; and yet it is danger
To make him even o'er[6] the time he has lost.
Desire him to go in; trouble him no more
Till further settling.

In *Macbeth,* two doctors are presented, an English physician and a Scottish physician. Macbeth, among his other characteristics, is an epileptic, and he has several fits during the play. The English doctor is consulted, and tells of the miraculous healing powers that monarchs were supposed to exert by 'touching'. He believes in witchcraft, and gives a good description of quackery, which must have been widespread in those days (*Macbeth,* IV, iii, 141):

Doctor. There are a crew of wretched souls
That stay his cure.[7] Their malady convinces
The great assay of art;[8] but at his touch,
Such sanctity hath heaven given his hand,
They presently amend.[9]

The second physician, a Scottish doctor, makes remarkable observations in the famous sleep-walking scene. It is no wonder that Lady Macbeth, with so many murders on her hands, walked in her sleep, for she must have had a very troubled subconscious mind. The doctor has been told about the lady's sleep-walking, but prefers to observe this phenomenon for himself (*Macbeth,* V, i, 1):

Doctor. I have two nights watch'd with you, but can perceive no truth in your report. When was it she last walk'd?

[23]

A lady-in-waiting to Lady Macbeth describes her actions and movements while asleep. The doctor then comments (V, i, 9):

> *Doctor.* A great perturbation in nature, to receive at once the benefit of sleep and do the effects of watching! In this slumb'ry agitation, besides her walking and other actual performances, what, at any time, have you heard her say?

The lady-in-waiting does not wish to confide in him without a third person being present – 'neither to you nor any one, having no witness to confirm my speech' – and he coaxes her:

> *Doctor.* You may to me; and 'tis most meet you should.

At this point, Lady Macbeth enters, sleep-walking, with eyes open, holding a lighted candle in her hand (V, i, 23):

> *Doctor.* You see her eyes are open.
> *Gentlewoman.* Ay, but their sense is shut.

He notes that she is rubbing her hands, a hand-washing obsession to clean them from the various foul misdemeanours she has perpetrated. Lady Macbeth speaks, and the doctor, realising the value of keeping notes to jog his memory, says (V, i, 31):

> *Doctor.* Hark, she speaks, I will set down what comes from her, to satisfy my remembrance the more strongly.

These are wise words, and keeping good notes is very important, even today. As the scene progresses, the doctor displays, in turn, scepticism, clinical interest, keen observation, concern for the patient's safety, and a desire to protect

A Medical Consultation, from Ketham's *Fasciculus Medicinae*,
1512. In the Middle Ages the doctor was often a person
with rank and academic connections, who would think of
disease in philosophical terms, rather than concentrating on
a cure. Here an assistant is presenting the urine for inspection.
(From *A History of Medicine* by A. Castiglioni, 1941.)

[25]

her confidences when their disclosure would place him in an ethical dilemma. However, he admits the case is beyond his capabilities, and turns her over to a higher authority, a 'divine' physician (V, i, 57):

> *Doctor.* This disease is beyond my practice. Yet I have known those which have walk'd in their sleep who have died holily in their beds.
>
>   ...
>
> *Doctor.* Foul whisp'rings are abroad. Unnatural deeds
> Do breed unnatural troubles; infected minds
> To their deaf pillows will discharge their secrets.
> More needs she the divine than the physician.
> God, God forgive us all. Look after her;
> Remove from her the means of all annoyance,[10]
> And still[11] keep eyes upon her. So, good night.
> My mind she has mated,[12] and amaz'd my sight.
> I think but dare not speak.

Concerned at his wife's deteriorating mental illness, Macbeth asks his physician (V, iii, 39):

>   Cure her of that.
> Canst thou not minister to a mind diseas'd,
> Pluck from the memory a rooted sorrow,
> Raze out the written troubles of the brain,
> And with some sweet oblivious antidote
> Cleanse the stuff'd bosom of that perilous stuff
> Which weighs upon the heart?

The wise doctor's reply is appropriate, and has often been endorsed by physicians of all ages:

> ... Therein the patient
> Must minister to himself.

To which Macbeth replies, in typical fashion:

Throw physic to the dogs – I'll none of it.

This is perhaps not so much a reflection of his contempt of medicine, as of his impatience at the doctor who stands irresolute and stubborn, when Macbeth is all for action.

Cornelius, the physician in *Cymbeline,* was actually something of an apothecary. He played with honour and astuteness a difficult part when the Queen asked him for a poison, and he found himself in an awkward situation, as he suspected that the Queen was likely to harm herself by an overdose of the drugs. She firmly believed that the drugs would kill her, but he called her bluff by selecting those which would dull her senses and bring about a deep sleep, but were not lethal (I, v, 4):

> *Queen.* Master doctor, have you brought those drugs?
> *Cornelius.* Pleaseth your Highness, ay. Here they are, madam.
> *[Presenting a box.]*
> But I beseech your Grace, without offence –
> My conscience bids me ask – wherefore you have
> Commanded of me these most poisonous compounds,
> Which are the movers[13] of a languishing death,
> But, though slow, deadly?
> *Queen.*   I wonder, Doctor,
> Thou ask'st me such a question. Have I not been
> Thy pupil long? Hast thou not learn'd me how
> To make perfumes? distil? preserve?
>   ...
>
>   I will try the forces
> Of these thy compounds on such creatures as

[27]

We count not worth the hanging – but none human –
To try the vigour of them, and apply
Allayments to their act, and by them gather
Their several virtues and effects.

   ...

Doctor, your service for this time is ended;
Take your own way.
Cornelius. [Aside] I do suspect you, madam;
But you shall do no harm.

   ...

                          She doth think she has
Strange ling'ring poisons. I do know her spirit,
And will not trust one of her malice with
A drug of such damn'd nature. Those she has
Will stupefy and dull the sense awhile,
Which first perchance she'll prove on cats and dogs,
Then afterward up higher; but there is
No danger in what show of death it makes,
More than the locking up the spirits a time,
To be more fresh, reviving. She is fool'd
With a most false effect; and I the truer
So to be false with her.
Queen.   No further service, Doctor,
Until I send for thee.
Cornelius.   I humbly take my leave.

Shakespeare wrote *Pericles, Prince of Tyre,* about the time of Dr John Hall's marriage to his daughter. Some believe that in this play he portrayed his son-in-law as Cerimon, so that the good social status of the medical man was here accepted and illustrated. Cerimon was not only a physician, but also a nobleman, a lord of Ephesus, and a mystic who was endowed with extraordinary healing powers. It is not

surprising therefore that Shakespeare's greatest tribute to
the medical profession is stated by Cerimon (*Pericles, III,* ii,
26):

Cerimon.   I hold it ever
Virtue and cunning [14] were endowments greater
Than nobleness and riches; careless heirs
May the two latter darken and expend;
But immortality attends the former,
Making a man a god. 'Tis known I ever
Have studied physic, through which secret art,
By turning o'er[15] authorities, I have,
Together with my practice, made familiar
To me and to my aid the blest infusions[16]
That dwell in vegetives,[17] in metals, stones;
And I can speak of the disturbances
That nature works, and of her cures; which doth give me
A more content in course of true delight,
Than to be thirsty after tottering honour,
Or tie my treasure up in silken bags,
To please the fool and death.
Gentleman. Your honour has through Ephesus pour'd forth
Your charity, and hundreds call themselves
Your creatures, who by you have been restor'd:
And not your knowledge, your personal pain, but even
Your purse, still open, hath built Lord Cerimon
Such strong renown as time shall never raze.

Sir William Butts, M.D. (died 1545), Fellow of Gonville
Hall, Cambridge, and of the Royal College of Physicians,
was physician to Henry VIII, and a leading physician of his
day. He was represented in Shakespeare's *King Henry VIII,* in

Thaisa (Stephanie Bidmead) and Cerimon
(Anthony Nicholls, to the right, standing); from
Act III, Scene II, of a production of *Pericles* by the
Shakespeare Memorial Theatre in 1958.
Photograph by Angus McBean, courtesy of The
Shakespeare Birthplace Trust.

which he has a very small part as physician to the king. On the other hand, in *All's Well That Ends Well,* Helena, the heroine of the play, is the daughter of Gerard de Narbon, a famous physician. The plot is founded on a medical problem. The King of France is seriously ill, suffering from a fistula,* which none of his physicians has been able to treat successfully.

He is cured by Helena, who learnt the secret remedy for this illness from her father before he died. A great deal of praise is lavished on Gerard de Narbon, who was represented as a highly skilled physician (I, i, 23):

Countess. He was famous, sir, in his profession, and it was his great right to be so – Gerard de Narbon.
Lafeu. He was excellent indeed, madam; the King very lately spoke of him admiringly and mournfully; he was skilful enough to have liv'd still, if knowledge could be set up against mortality.[18]

Helena describes the knowledge her father imparted to her (I, iii, 212):

Helena. You know my father left me some prescriptions
Of rare and prov'd effects, such as his reading
And manifest experience had collected ...

Bertram. What is it, my good lord, the King languishes of?
Lafeu. A fistula, my lord.
Bertram. I heard not of it before. (*All's Well, That Ends Well,* I, i, 29)

She undertakes to treat and cure the king with her father's secret remedy, and eventually succeeds in doing so. However, the king and his court are sceptical of her talents, especially as the Royal College of Physicians ('congregated college')* had given its verdict that the King's illness was incurable (II, i, 114):

> *King.*   We thank you, maiden;
> But may not be so credulous of cure,
> When our most learned doctors leave us, and
> The congregated college[19] have concluded
> That labouring art can never ransom nature
> From her inaidable estate[20] – I say we must not
> So stain our judgment, or corrupt our hope,
> To prostitute our past-cure malady
> To empirics;[21] or to dissever so
> Our great self and our credit to esteem
> A senseless help, when help past sense we deem.

Shakespeare has many fine words for members of the medical profession – for instance, the words of Julius Caesar (*Julius Caesar I*, ii, 201):

> He reads much,
> He is a great observer, and he looks
> Quite through the deeds of men.

---

*The Royal College of Physicians of London was founded in 1518 by Henry VIII, with the object of controlling irregular and unlearned medical practice. He was persuaded to do this by Thomas Linacre, one of his own physicians, to follow the example of similar institutions in Italy and elsewhere.

Another example comes from *All's Well That Ends Well* (V, iii, 101):

King of France.   Plutus* himself
That knows the tinct and multiplying med'cine[22]
Hath not in nature's mystery more science[23]

Shakespeare also draws attention to their professed intention to cure:

Abbess. Be patient; for I will not let him stir
Till I have us'd the approved means I have,
With wholesome syrups, drugs and holy prayers,
To make of him a formal[24] man again.
It is a branch and parcel of mine oath,
A charitable duty of my order ...

Comedy of Errors, V, i, 102

Ligarius. Thou, like an exorcist, hast conjur'd up
My mortified[25] spirit. Now bid me run,
And I will strive with things impossible;
Yea, get the better of them.

Julius Caesar, II, i, 323

Generally, Shakespeare spoke of physicians and medical matters with respect; but he also had a fling at doctors, as the following passages will show:

Pericles. Thou speak'st like a physician, Helicanus,
That ministers a potion unto me

---

*Plutus: the god of wealth in Greek mythology, who was blinded so that he would give riches to good and bad people alike. He is often shown lame (because wealth comes slowly), or with wings (to show that money flies away fast).

That thou wouldst tremble to receive thyself.

Pericles, I, ii, 67

And:

Cornelius.   Hail, great King!
To sour your happiness I must report
The Queen is dead.
Cymbeline.   Who worse than a physician
Would this report become? But I consider
By med'cine life may be prolong'd, yet death
Will seize the doctor too.

Cymbeline, V, v, 25

And again:

Sempronius. Must I be his last refuge? His friends, like physicians,
Thrice give him over. Must I take th' cure upon me?

Timon, III, iii, II

There are situations in which a patient knows that his physician can do no more. This is expressed in *All's Well That Ends Well* by those attending on the sick king: (I, i, 12):

Lafeu. He hath abandon'd his physicians, madam; under whose practices he hath persecuted time with hope,[26] and finds no other advantage in the process but only the losing of hope by time.

And (I, iii, 228):

Countess.   He and his physicians
Are of a mind: he, that they cannot help him;
They, that they cannot help.

He also had a few useful words for those who specialised

in high fees and charged their patients too much:

> *Thersites.*.... lose all the serpentine craft of thy caduceus,* if ye take not that little less-than-little wit from them that they have!
>
> Troilus and Cressida, II, iii, 14

> *Kent.* Kill thy physician, and the fee bestow
> Upon the foul disease.
>
> Lear, I, i, 163

We would of course always prefer our patients to have the view: 'I, thy resolv'd patient, on thee still rely' (*All's Well, that Ends Well,* II, i, 202). However, a patient's opinion is often summed up in these few words, frequently appropriate:

> *Host.* Shall I lose my doctor? No;
> he gives me the potions and the motions.
>
> The Merry Wives of Windsor, III, i, 94

---

*The caduceus was the magic wand given by Apollo to Mercury, the messenger of the gods. Mercury used it to guide the souls of the dead to the lower world. It had wings at its top and snakes entwined around it. It is now an emblem of the medical profession.

H. Beerbohm Tree as Malvolio in *Twelfth Night*
(Act II, Scene V); from *The Complete Works of
William Shakespeare* (c. 1910). Photograph: R.
Caswall Smith, London.

2
MENTAL ILLNESS

Polonius. Mad call I it; for, to define true madness,
What is't but to be nothing else but mad?
Hamlet, Prince of Denmark, II, ii, 93

HE NATURAL HISTORY OF MENTAL ILLNESS
has from the earliest times been the subject
of much study and of much controversy. A
famous text on this subject was published
by Robert Burton in 1621. This was *The
Anatomy of Melancholy,* in which he approached the problem
in a more or less scientific manner, classifying melancholy
according to its various manifestations, and then proceeding
from symptoms and signs to differential diagnosis, prognosis
and treatment. His description of melancholy (which is
depression as we know it today) is almost as good now as it
was 350 years ago:

> Although they be commonly lean, hirsute, uncheerful in
> countenance, withered and not so pleasant to behold, by
> reason of those continual fears, griefs and vexations, dull,
> heavy, lazy, restless, unapt to go about any business: yet their
> memories are most part good ...
> Fear and sorrow are no common symptoms to all melancholy.
> I find some that are not so at all. Some indeed are sad and not
> fearful ...

Burton's text was one of the best known, and he lumped
together as melancholy a wide range of mental attitudes

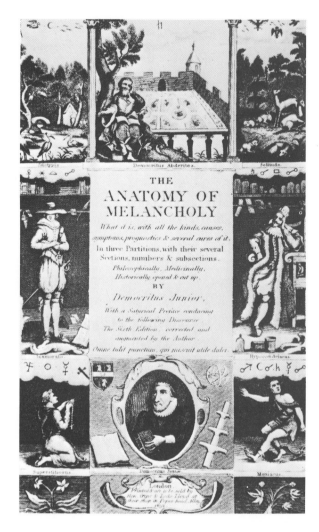

Title page of *The Anatomy of Melancholy* by Robert
Burton (sixth edition, 1652). Sir William Osler
considered this the greatest contribution to psychiatry
by a layman. It is an excellent account of
depression, and provides some perceptive insights,
such as the benefits of sharing grief with a friend.

extending from a mild eccentric disorder to an established neurosis and even the wildest psychotic derangement. There was, however, an earlier *Treatise on Melancholy* published in 1586 by Timothy Bright, a resident physician of St Bartholomew's Hospital, London. There have been suggestions that Shakespeare had some acquaintance with Bright's *Treatise*, and that he drew on the information in this book to create his psychological delineations. They are many, and cover the whole range from mental perversion (in *Titus Andronicus**), and the foolish imbecility of characters like Simple, Shallow and Speed, to the dementia and madness of Lear.

Many sufferers from mental depression (or 'melancholia') have some degree of insight into their illness and are aware of their problems. For these people Shakespeare's powers of observation, and his unique ability to translate these into words, are seen in several instances, including the opening lines of *The Merchant of Venice*. Antonio, the merchant, is melancholic; he does not know why and is unable to shake off the mood:

> In sooth, I know not why I am so sad.
> It wearies me; you say it wearies you;
> But how I caught it, found it, or came by it,
> What stuff 'tis made of, whereof it is born,
> I am to learn;
> And such a want-wit sadness makes of me
> That I have much ado to know myself.

Titus Andronicus was Shakespeare's first tragedy, and considered by some as his worst play, because it is heavily loaded with gore, murder, rape, mutilation, severed heads and hands, and so on.

'A Rake's Progress', by William Hogarth (1763). Bedlam prevails
in the conditions shown in London's Bethlehem Hospital.
Sightseers were permitted to view the insane for a small charge.
Shakespeare made many references to 'Bedlam'.

Also, a further expression of his depression (I, i, 77):

I hold the world but as the world, Gratiano –
A stage, where every man must play a part,
And mine a sad one.

And in *Love's Labour's Lost* (V, ii, 725) we read:

Princess. A heavy heart bears not a nimble tongue.

Severely depressed patients, however, in a state of deep

mental distress, as with patients with other psychoses, often suffer from a defect in judgement or reason which makes them almost indifferent to their illness or the need for treatment. This feeling of deep depression is expressed by Belarius when he finds that his beloved Imogen is dead (*Cymbeline*, IV, ii, 204):

> O melancholy!
> Who ever yet could sound thy bottom?

Neurotic persons are more likely to suffer from emotional or psychological defects, and sometimes, these may be accompanied by obsessions or delusions. Frequent washing of the hands 'to clean them' has always been one of the more common obsessions. Lady Macbeth, a high-class murderess, expressed her sufferings from this neurotic disorder *(Macbeth,* II, ii, 60, and V, i, 41, 48):

> Will all great Neptune's ocean wash this blood
> Clean from my hand?
> . . .
>
> What, will these hands ne'er be clean?
> . . .
>
> Here's the smell of the blood still. All the perfumes of Arabia will not sweeten this little hand.

It was not surprising that Macbeth also exhibited some mental disturbance. In this case (II, i, 38), he had a delusion about the murder weapon, a dagger:

> Is this a dagger which I see before me,
>   . . . or art thou but
> A dagger of the mind, a false creation,
> Proceeding from the heat-oppressed brain?

Shakespeare made many references to depression in his plays. We now distinguish the reactive from the endogenous depressions, and with respect to the reactive types, of which some circumstances in the environment are a precipitating cause, he also made a few observations. Timon (*Timon*, IV, iii, 201), is told by Apemantus, a philosopher, that his melancholy is derived from a change in his circumstances:

> This is in thee a nature but infected,
> A poor unmanly melancholy sprung
> From change of fortune.

In *The Comedy of Errors* (V, i, 78) we read:

> *Lady Abbess.* Sweet recreation barr'd,[1] what doth ensue
> But moody and dull melancholy ...

In endogenous depression, however, there may be no apparent precipitating cause, and a patient may slip deeper and deeper into its depths, losing interest in all around him, and at the same time having a preoccupation with grief, sadness, and death. *King Richard II* is a drama woven around the failure and death of a king, and Richard's tragedy is not that he came to misery and death, but that he brought on his own destruction (III, ii, 144):

> *King Richard.* No matter where – of comfort no man speak.
> Let's talk of graves, of worms, and epitaphs;
> Make dust our paper, and with rainy eyes
> Write sorrow on the bosom of the earth.
> Let's choose executors and talk of wills;
> And yet not so – for what can we bequeath
> Save our deposed bodies to the ground?

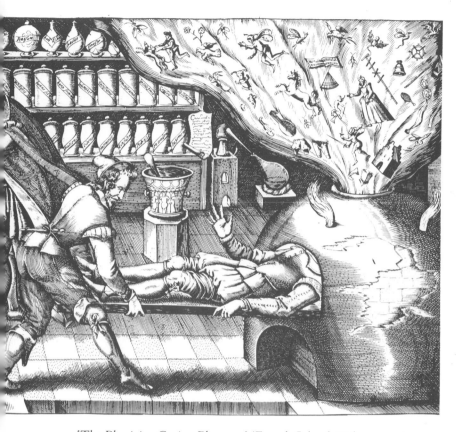

'The Physician Curing Phantasy' (French School, 17th century). Reproduced from *Medicine and the Artist (Ars Medica)* by permission of the Philadelphia Museum of Art; Dover Publications, Inc., New York.

The other common psychoses as we know them today – schizophrenia, paranoia, organic psychosis and psychopathic personality disorders – were obviously not defined in Shakespeare's time; they have been classified comparatively recently. Even now, the experts and others will disagree on their classification. They were then all lumped together as lunacy, madness or insanity. Insanity is as old as history, and asylums for the insane were in existence from about the thirteenth century, but were far from being hospitals where the patient's mental state was being treated. Bethlehem Hospital ('Bedlam') in London was one of the earliest, and it received lunatics from 1377 onwards. An inventory of its equipment, twenty years later, included manacles, irons, chains, locks and keys, stocks, and other such restraining apparatus. Fortunately, over the centuries, these have been replaced with padded cells, the straitjacket, and of course more recently, the psychotherapeutic drugs. In those days, a visit to Bedlam to observe the lunatics was a visit to one of the sights of London. Brutus (*Julius Caesar*, II, i, 63), describes the various and differing mental states with which man can be afflicted:

> Between the acting of a dreadful thing
> And the first motion, all the interim is
> Like a phantasma or a hideous dream.[2]
> The Genius and the mortal instruments
> Are then in council; and the state of man,
> Like to a little kingdom, suffers then
> The nature of an insurrection.[3]

Hamlet's mental state is described by his mother, the Queen (IV, i, 7):

> Mad as the sea and wind, when both contend
> Which is the mightier.

Macbeth had a troubled mind when he told his wife (III, ii, 36):

> O, full of scorpions is my mind . . .

A treatment of insanity. In the Middle Ages the usual treatment was to confine the patient in a dark room, often restrained. Another method was that shown here, the 'hunger method', in which hungry patients were suspended over the dining table. (Roback, A. A., and Kiernan, T., N.Y. Philosophical Library, 1969.)

'Melancholy', a copper engraving made by
Albrecht Dürer in 1514. It admirably depicts
woman in severe depression.

And in *The Tempest* (I, ii, 214) we read:

Ariel. Hell is empty,
And all the devils are here.

Getting away from the organic psychoses, some of the commoner and possibly more vaguely defined neuroses have also been touched upon in some plays – hysteria and hypochondria, for example. The latter is described by Lear (II, iv, 105) in the earlier stages of his progressive deterioration:

... we are not ourselves
When nature, being oppress'd, commands the mind
To suffer with the body.

The word 'lunatic' (*luna* = moon) about this time implied an intermittent form of insanity occasioned by changes in the phases of the moon. This belief in varying degrees still exists today. Othello, when advised by Emilia, Iago's wife, that a murder has been committed, alludes to the lunar theory of insanity (V, ii, 112):

It is the very error of the moon;
She comes more nearer earth than she was wont,
And makes men mad.

Unfortunately, mental illness in old age is often associated with cerebral dementia. King Lear's illness is an example of progressive mental deterioration ending in senile dementia; the same condition is described overleaf by Prince Henry in relation to his dying father, King John, as 'idle comments', or demented speech (*King John,* V, vii, 1):

It is too late; the life of all his blood
Is touch'd corruptibly, and his pure brain,
Which some suppose the soul's frail dwelling-house,
Doth by the idle comments that it makes
Foretell the ending of mortality.

Whereas there is no effective treatment for senile dementia, the treatment of some anxiety neuroses is largely psychological. The problem can be made difficult when the origin of the illness is obscure:

Montague. Could we but learn from whence his sorrows grow,
We would as willingly give cure as know.

Romeo and Juliet, I, i, 152

The treatment and understanding of mental illness evolved slowly. If anything went wrong with the mind, the devil offered a ready explanation. Ordinary diseases might have natural causes, but mental disorders, because of the abnormal behaviour of the sufferers, were often attributed to the maleficence of sorcerers and witches, who were the agents of the evil one. Divine aid was thus frequently resorted to, on the basis that mental illness was perhaps the result of an evil visitation. King Henry VI offers a prayer for a dying Cardinal, the Bishop of Winchester (2 *King Henry VI,* III, iii, 19):

O Thou eternal Mover of the heavens,
Look with a gentle eye upon this wretch!
O, beat away the busy meddling fiend
That lays strong siege unto this wretch's soul,
And from his bosom purge this black despair!

Dr Pilch (James Booth), Adriana (Diana Rigg), Antipholus of Ephesus
(Ian Richardson), and Dromio of Ephesus (Ian Hewitson), in a
production of *The Comedy of Errors* by the Royal Shakespeare Theatre
in 1962. Photograph by Gordon Goode, reproduced by courtesy of The
Shakespeare Birthplace Trust, Shakespeare Centre Library.

In *The Comedy of Errors* (IV, iv, 51) Pinch, a schoolmaster,
makes this attempt at exorcising the devil:

I charge thee, Satan, hous'd within this man,
To yield possession to my holy prayers,
And to thy state of darkness hie thee straight,
I conjure thee by all the saints in Heaven.

[49]

Galen at the Bedside (from a 1586 edition of his
works). He is observing a lady whose illness was
not due to physical causes, but to unrequited love,
as can be seen by her expression. (From the
National Library of Medicine, Bethesda.)

However, the usual treatment in those mediaeval days was a comparatively simple matter. Perhaps it was only the grossly agitated types that were treated at all, for the safety of the public. The usual method was to confine the unfortunate person to a dark room, often restrained. Again, the energetic Pinch suggests this method (IV, iv, 89):

> Mistress, both man and master is possess'd
> I know it by their pale and deadly looks.
> They must be bound, and laid in some dark room.

In *Twelfth Night,* Sir Toby Belch, referring to Malvolio, says: 'Come, we'll have him in a dark room and bound.' In *As You Like It,* Rosalind in a word-play with Orlando, says: 'love is merely a madness; and, I tell you, deserves as well a dark house and a whip as madmen do.' Again, when the Abbess in *The Comedy Of Errors* asks Adriana what she has come for, Adriana replies (V, i, 40):

> To fetch my poor distracted husband hence.
> Let us come in, that we may bind him fast,
> And bear him home for his recovery.

The Abbess later objects (V, i, 101):

> Be patient; for I will not let him stir
> Till I have us'd the approved means I have,
> With wholesome syrups, drugs, and holy prayers,
> To make of him a formal[4] man again.

Benvolio, surprised at Romeo's melancholy, exclaims 'Why, Romeo, art thou mad?' to which Romeo retorts 'Not mad, but bound more than a madman is'.

Music and merrymaking would help some patients with disturbed minds:

> *Messenger.* For so your doctors hold it very meet,
> Seeing too much sadness hath congeal'd your blood,
> And melancholy is the nurse of frenzy.[5]
> Therefore they thought it good you hear a play
> And frame your mind to mirth and merriment,
> Which bars a thousand harms and lengthens life.
>
> *Taming of the Shrew,* Ind. ii, 128

However, music might also have the reverse effect:

> *King Richard.* This music mads me. Let it sound no more;
> For though it have holp[6] madmen to their wits,
> In me it seems it will make wise men mad.
>
> *King Richard II,* V, v, 61

A sympathetic ear and kind words are the basis of good psychotherapy, and this was foreseen by a sympathetic Paulina pleading on behalf of another person in trouble *(The Winter's Tale,* II, iii, 37):

> ...I
> Do come with words as medicinal[7] as true,
> Honest as either, to purge him of that humour.[8]

It was also foreseen by Romeo's father, Montague *(Romeo and Juliet* I, i, 139):

> Black and portentous must this humour prove,
> Unless good counsel may the cause remove.

Hamlet, Prince of Denmark is considered to be Shakespeare's greatest play, and possibly one of the most interesting ever written. There is one remarkable passage in

Hamlet which is given below. In this, Hamlet has used the word 'complexion', and if we take this to mean 'complexes', then it was a term which remained dormant in the psychological sense until resurrected by Freud 300 years later (*Hamlet*, I, iv, 23):

> So, oft if chances in particular men
> That, for some vicious mole[9] of nature in them,
> As in their birth, wherein they are not guilty,
> Since nature cannot choose his origin;
> By the o'ergrowth of some complexion,*
> Oft breaking down the pales[10] and forts of reason;
> Or by some habit that too much o'erleavens[11]
> The form of plausive[12] manners – that these men,
> Carrying, I say, the stamp of one defect,
> Being nature's livery[13] or fortune's star,[14]
> His virtues else, be they as pure as grace,
> As infinite as man may undergo,
> Shall in the general censure take corruption
> From that particular fault.

---

*o' ergrowth of some complexion: some quality allowed to overbalance the rest, 'complexion' meaning 'complexes' – psychological complexes.

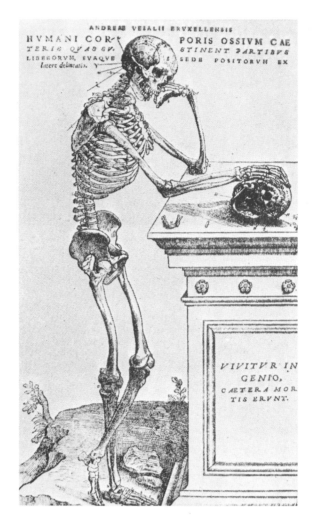

The Skeleton in Meditation, from *De humani corporis fabrica* by Andreas Vesalius. This picture is believed to have been the inspiration for Shakespeare's character Hamlet. (From *A History of Medicine* by A. Castiglioni, 1941.)

3
THE MADNESS OF
LEAR, HAMLET & TIMON

Theseus. The lunatic, the lover and the poet,
Are of imagination all compact.
One sees more devils than vast hell can hold;
That is the madman.
                    A Midsummer Night's Dream, V, i, 7

Ariel.   Hell is empty,
And all the devils are here.
                         The Tempest, I, ii, 214

HAKESPEARE'S PLAYS contain very many references to a disturbed state of mind. He must have had a profound understanding of human nature, because he depicted his observations of disordered mental states in several famous characters. He probably had many opportunities of observing the peculiar qualities of the mentally deranged. In his day, only the dangerously insane were confined to institutions or asylums. Some were even jailed, and as his father was chamberlain in the local council and bailiff for many years at Stratford, this may have provided opportunities for him to observe these people at first hand. His daughter Susanna, married to Dr John Hall the physician, suffered from a neurosis which was possibly a complication of scurvy, for Dr Hall wrote about her in his notes: 'Observation XXXIII: Wife was troubled with the scurvy accompanied with ... melancholy, wind, cardiac passion,

laziness, difficulty in breathing, fear ...'*

Although Shakespeare paid special attention to the abnormal mental states – and many characters in his plays are shown to suffer from them – these descriptions were not peculiar to him. Evidently the Elizabethan audience enjoyed seeing madmen on the stage, and many contemporary playwrights introduced maniacs and imbeciles into their dramas. All of these types, and more, are represented among Shakespeare's characters. We thus read of the melancholy of Jaques, the hallucinations of Macbeth and the somnabulism of Lady Macbeth. Other mentally affected characters are Caliban, Bottom the weaver, Malvolio, Launcelot Gobbo, Touchstone and Sir Andrew Aguecheek. Othello was racked by jealousy until his senses almost gave way, and though it did not drive him to madness it did to suicide.

In those days, madmen were even exhibited in asylums for a penny or two admission, and this must have given Shakespeare further scope to study various psychological delineations. Many of these unfortunate people were known as 'Bedlam beggars' (*Lear,* II, iii, 14); 'Bedlam' or 'Bethlehem' was a common name for the Hospital of St Mary of Bethlehem in London, which was used as an asylum for the mentally deranged. Shakespeare refers to Bedlam several times:

King John. Bedlam have done
Constance.   I have but this to say –

---

*British Museum Egerton MSS 2065, Dr John Hall in his 'Select Observations on English Bodies'.

[56]

That he is not only plagued for her sin ...
King John, II, i, 183

Pistol. Ha! Art thou bedlam?
King Henry V, V, i, 18

Clifford. To Bedlam with him! Is the man grown mad?
King. Ay, Clifford; a bedlam and ambitious humour[1]
Makes him oppose himself against his king.
2 King Henry VI, V, i, 131

Suffolk. And such high vaunts of his nobility,
Did instigate the bedlam brainsick Duchess
By wicked means to frame[2] our sovereign's fall.
2 King Henry VI, III, i, 50

Edmund. My cue is villainous melancholy, with a sigh like Tom
o'Bedlam.[3]
King Lear, I, ii, 129
2 Servant. Let's follow the old Earl and get the Bedlam
To lead him where he would. His roughish madness
Allows itself to anything.
King Lear, III, vii, 102

In the following account of Bedlam (*King Lear*, II, iii, 13),
Shakespeare describes the actions of some unfortunate
inmates, who were reduced to begging and mutilating
themselves with pins and other objects in order to attract
attention:

Edgar. The country gives me proof and precedent[4]
Of Bedlam beggars, who, with roaring voices,
Strike in their numb'd and mortified[5] bare arms
Pins, wooden bricks, nails, sprigs of rosemary;
And with this horrible object, from low[6] farms,

[57]

Poor pelting[7] villages, sheep-cotes, and mills,
Sometimes with lunatic bans,[8] sometime with prayers,
Enforce their charity.

KING LEAR

Shakespeare further portrayed the borderline between madness and normality, the uncertain state of mind between sanity and insanity, and from these situations he produced some famous characters in his more popular tragedies. So skilfully are these characters developed that those studying them from different points of view may find that there is a complete expression of their own conceptions. King Lear, for instance, can be described as an example of mental deterioration in a man in whom the disorder can be traced step by step. He is an old man of violent temper, with no reserve of emotion or restraint. Like an Old Testament prophet, he denounces his daughter Goneril, and then goes further, at first praying that she be childless ('Into her womb convey sterility'), and later asking Nature for her to bear an ungrateful child, so that she may know what it is to have a thankless child: 'How sharper than a serpent's tooth it is to have a thankless child!' The first signs of mental distress are noticed by Lear himself (I, iv, 271):

Beat at this gate,[9] that let thy folly in
And thy dear judgement out! [*Striking his head*]

From the beginning of the play, we read that Lear's mind is unsound, and many have considered him as portraying a case of progressive senile dementia. This is accompanied by attacks of what could be described today as acute mania, which are demonstrated by his faulty judgement, disorientation and irrational behaviour (IV, i, 47; IV, iv, 2):

> Gloucester. 'Tis the times' plague[10] when madmen lead the blind
> ...
>
> Cordelia. As mad as the vex'd sea ...

At the same time, he tries hard to maintain control of himself (I, v, 43):

Lear. O, let me not be mad, not mad, sweet heaven!
Keep me in temper; ...

From his first appearance to the last, Lear appears deprived of reason. Passage after passage emphasises the degradation to which man can sink; it is summed up in one terrible line (IV, vi, 159): '... a dog's obeyed in office.' Lear was not even obeyed; worse still, he was mocked and scorned.

The scenes in which Lear, Edgar, Kent and Lear's fool seek refuge together from a storm are among the most harrowing in Shakespeare's plays. His apparent failure to suffer physical discomfort while exposed to the storm represents a state in which his disturbed mind has reduced the body's sensibility to pain and discomfort (III, iv, 11):

> Lear.   When the mind's free[11]
> The body's delicate; this tempest in my mind
> Doth from my senses take all feeling else,
> Save what beats there.

The tragedy of King Lear is a description of ingratitude – an ingratitude that divides parent from child and splits human relationships. The infiltration of Lear's mind by the ingratitude of his daughters also shows points of psychological interest, (III, vi, 104):

> *Edgar.* Who alone suffers suffers most i' th' mind,
> Leaving free things and happy shows behind;
> But then the mind much sufferance doth o'erskip
> When grief hath mates, and bearing fellowship.[12]

Shakespeare described Lear's fear of insanity, a symptom possibly felt by some in a similar state of mind (IV, vii, 63):

> *Lear.* I fear I am not in my perfect mind.

In Act I his 'discernings are lethargised'; soon his memory begins to fail; he becomes 'talkative', he shows a 'wayward pettiness'. As early as the fifth scene he foresees and fears an impending madness, and in Act II he senses the beginning of 'hysterica passio':

> *Lear.* O, how this mother swells up toward my heart!
> Hysterica passio – down, thou climbing sorrow,
> Thy element's below.*

In Act III his 'wits begin to turn', and he complains of 'melancholy' and 'cold', and the Fool prophetically declares: 'This cold night will turn us all to fools and madmen!' By the end of the act Lear's wits are 'gone'. In Act IV he is 'mad', and imagines Kent and Edgar as judges in a court condemning his two older daughters. Towards the end of

---

*The 'mother', also called *hysterica passio*, was an overwhelming feeling of physical distress and suffocation. Lear's mental suffering is now beginning to cause a physical breakdown. This sensation, and the violent throbbing of the heart until finally it ceases, can be traced in Lear's speeches (II, iv, 119, 134, 196; III, iv, 12).

Act IV, his cure begins by the medically accepted means of music and complete rest. But the defeat of Cordelia brings on the final tragedy of his death. Lear brings much suffering on himself by his own stupidity. The final stages of progressive senility ending in dementia are briefly described by Kent, his one faithful follower (III, vi, 87):

... trouble him not – his wits are gone.

Thus, Lear's deterioration is a case history of senile dementia, of mental and physical decay, brought on and aggravated by misfortune and advancing years.

HAMLET

In Hamlet, Shakespeare portrayed a different state of mental disorder – a feigned psychosis in a weak and indecisive individual with marked depressive overtones. This element of feigned insanity is typical of Hamlet (I, v, 171).

Hamlet. As I perchance hereafter shall think meet
To put an antic disposition[13] on –

And (II, ii, 203):

Polonius. Though this be madness, yet there is method in 't –

From this is derived the much-used aphorism 'method in his madness'.

Hamlet also exhibits some characteristic features of depression, such as self-denial and suicidal thoughts. It is mainly the reaction of his mother's marriage to his father's brother that precipitates his abnormal mental state. He is sorrowful and full of sadness with 'nighted colour' and 'inky cloak', and is asked by his stepfather, the King of Denmark (I, ii, 66): "How is it that the clouds still hang on you?" He describes his depressed mood to his mother, stressing the point that he is not feigning sadness (I, ii, 77):

'Tis not alone my inky cloak, good mother,
Nor customary suits of solemn black,
Nor windy suspiration of forc'd breath,
No, nor the fruitful river[14] in the eye,
Nor the dejected haviour of the visage,[15]
Together with all forms, moods, shapes of grief,
That can denote me truly. These, indeed, seem;
For they are actions that a man might play;[16]
But I have that within which passes show –
These but the trappings[17] and the suits of woe.

Shakespeare must have known that suicidal thoughts are indeed an unfortunate accompaniment of the severely depressed mind, and accordingly expressed Hamlet's death wish and thoughts of suicide as follows (I, ii, 129):

O, that this too too solid flesh would melt,
Thaw, and resolve itself into a dew!
Or that the Everlasting had not fix'd
His canon[18] 'gainst self-slaughter! O God! God!
How weary, stale, flat, and unprofitable,
Seem to me all the uses of this world!
Fie on't! Ah, fie! 'tis an unweeded garden
That grows to seed; things rank and gross in nature
Possess it merely.

Hamlet's contemplation of suicide is firmly expressed in the well-known soliloquy (III, i, 56):

Hamlet. To be, or not to be – that is the question;
Whether 'tis nobler in the mind to suffer
The slings and arrows of outrageous[19] fortune,
Or to take arms against a sea[20] of troubles,
And by opposing[21] end them? To die, to sleep –
No more; and by a sleep to say we end
The heart-ache and the thousand natural shocks
That flesh is heir to. 'Tis a consummation[22]
Devoutly to be wish'd.

However, Hamlet expressed the fear of the unknown, the uncertainty of taking that fatal step because of what might befall him in the next world (III, i, 76):

Who would these fardels[23] bear,
To grunt and sweat under a weary life,
But that the dread of something after death –
The undiscover'd country, from whose bourn[24]
No traveller returns – puzzles the will,[25]
And makes us rather bear those ills we have
Than fly to others that we know not of?

Insomnia, a common symptom of depression, is also mentioned. Hamlet describes his palpitation ('a kind of fighting' in the heart) which was the cause of his insomnia (V, ii, 4):

Sir, in my heart there was a kind of fighting
That would not let me sleep.

Some opinions on mental disorder, in their broadest sense, are expressed by three leading characters in this play:

Polonius.   . . . to define true madness
What is't but to be nothing else but mad?
(II, ii, 93)

King. Madness in great ones must not unwatch'd go.
(III, i, 188) .

Queen. Mad as the sea and wind, when both contend
Which is the mightier.
(IV, i, 7)

It is unusual for all the symptoms of a disease to appear at the same time in a person suffering from that disease. On this basis, we can assume that Shakespeare presented Hamlet as a mentally ill and depressed individual, with the disease 'melancholia', which had been well recognized as a fairly common complaint. We know that Hamlet had no organic symptoms; for example, he had no fever, his 'pulse temporarily' kept 'time', his 'sadness' was 'without any apparent occasion'. There was something 'within which passeth show', 'the heart of his mystery', the 'loss of his mirth' and his going 'heavily' with his 'disposition'. All these are among the many symptoms of depression, either reactive or endogenous, as we know them today.

TIMON OF ATHENS

In *Timon of Athens* a different mental disorder is presented. Timon is a man whose generosity and extravagance outstrip his capacity to provide. He is a rich Athenian who spends lavishly on his friends and acquaintances. When he runs out of money and is in difficulties, he approaches those on whom he formerly lavished gifts, only to receive rebuffs. Disillusioned and soured, he invites his false friends to a 'banquet', at which nothing is served but warm water, and he throws this into their faces! Finally, he withdraws to live as a hermit in the woods, sick in mind and grossly affected by his change in circumstances (IV, iii, 202):

> *Apemantus.* This is in thee a nature but infected,
> A poor unmanly melancholy sprung
> From change of fortune.

Throughout the play, Timon behaves as a person deprived of reason, without insight into his actions and suffering a mental disturbance of gross dimensions. Strangely, Shakespeare makes more references to the spread of syphilis in *Timon of Athens* than in any other play. He has exhibited, in various passages, considerable knowledge of the symptoms, complications and consequences of syphilis. Is it possible that Shakespeare portrayed Timon as a rich man whose body and brain were affected by the late or tertiary stages of syphilis? This disease – namely, general paralysis of the insane – is now rare, but was common in the last three centuries preceding the penicillin era.

There are many references in *Timon of Athens* to the spread of syphilis from prostitutes, an association which was as well known then as it is now. Timon speaks like an expert:

> Be a whore still; they love thee not that use thee.
> Give them diseases, leaving with thee their lust.
> Make use of thy salt[26] hours. Season[27] the slaves
> For tubs and baths;[28] bring down rose-cheek'd youth
> To the tub-fast and diet.
>
> (IV, iii, 82)

> She whom the spital-house[29] and ulcerous sores
> Would cast the gorge at . . .[30]
>
> (IV, iii, 39)

> This fell[31] whore of thine
> Hath in her more destruction than thy sword
> For all her cherubin look.
> *Phrynia.*
>   Thy lips rot off!
> *Timon.* I will not kiss thee; then the rot returns
> To thine own lips again.
>   (IV, iii, 60)

Timon's behaviour could be described as total irresponsibility, a symptom which occurs in syphilitic disease of the nervous system. This condition is portrayed in Timon perhaps in the way in which Shakespeare saw it in others so affected. Venereal disease was extremely prevalent in London at that time, and many brothels were situated in the area surrounding the theatres of the South Bank, an area where Shakespeare lived and where many of his plays were enacted.

Timon, in his speeches, calls down epidemics of dreadful diseases – a senseless, irrational tirade; an insane commentary such as one would expect from a man with an organic disease of the brain (IV, i, 3):

>   ...Matrons, turn incontinent.
> Obedience, fail in children! Slaves and fools,
> Pluck the grave wrinkled Senate from the bench
> And minister in their steads. To general filths[32]
> Convert, o' the instant, green virginity.
> Do't in your parents' eyes. Bankrupts, hold fast;[33]
> Rather than render back, out with your knives
> And cut your trusters' throats. Bound servants,[34] steal:
> Large-handed robbers your grave masters are,
> And pill[35] by law. Maid, to thy master's bed:
> Thy mistress is o' the brothel. Son of sixteen,
> Pluck the lin'd[36] crutch from thy old limping sire,

With it beat out his brains. Piety and fear,
Religion to the gods, peace, justice, truth,
Domestic awe,[37] night-rest, and neighbourhood,[38]
Instruction, manners, mysteries[39] and trades,
Degrees, observances, customs and laws,
Decline[40] to your confounding contraries[41]
And let confusion live. Plagues incident to men,
Your potent and infectious fevers heap
On Athens, ripe for stroke. Thou cold sciatica,
Cripple our Senators, that their limbs may halt[42]
As lamely as their manners! Lust and liberty,[43]
Creep in the minds and marrows of our youth,
That 'gainst the stream of virtue they may strive
And drown themselves in riot. Itches, blains,[44]
Sow all th' Athenian bosoms, and their crop
Be general leprosy! Breath infect breath,
That their society, as their friendship, may
Be merely[45] poison!

Shakespeare thus portrayed the intellectual deterioration, the personality changes and the progressive loss of the higher cerebral faculties which are typical of general paralysis of the insane. This illness was described in 1798 by John Haslam, an apothecary at Bethlehem Hospital, and from then onwards was increasingly suspected by physicians as a late syphilitic manifestation. Was Timon a 'general paretic'? Shakespeare recorded various signs and symptoms in Timon which in his day were a common enough sight. No more vivid clinical picture of the tertiary stages of syphilis has ever been written than Timon's advice to two prostitutes on how to take revenge on men by infecting them with syphilis! (IV, iii, 150-163). Was Timon instructing them on the symptoms and signs of the disease from which he suffered?

A Camp Follower. These women were largely
responsible for the spread of syphilis, since they
moved freely between the camps of the
antagonists.

4

VENEREAL DISEASE 'THE POX'

YPHILIS FIRST appeared in Europe at about the time when Columbus returned from the New World (1492). It spread over the whole of Europe after the French armies, under Charles VIII of France, invaded Italy to seize the throne of Naples. His army consisted of many Spanish mercenaries, and, when they laid siege to Naples, they were accompanied by a large collection of female camp-followers who moved impartially between besiegers and defenders. The King of Naples also had his share of Spanish mercenaries, and by 1495 the plague had affected both the attackers and the defenders. The new disease, syphilis, which now appeared in a most virulent form, was so severe that it forced Charles to abandon his siege and retreat from Italy. Sexually transmissible, it passed with great rapidity from man to woman, and then to another man and another woman. As the people of various countries in Europe became infected, each put the blame for the new and terrifying disease on its neighbour or opponent. The French, who were affected in 1495, called it the 'Italian disease', and the Italians called it the 'Spanish disease'. By 1495-96 it had spread throughout Europe, and it reached England in 1497,

where it was called the 'French disease'.

The name 'syphilis' was first given to the disease in 1530, when Fracastoro, * a physician of Verona, wrote a poem called *Syphilis sive morbus Gallicus* ('Syphilis or the French Disease'). Fracastoro studied medicine at the University of Padua and was also something of an astrologer, philosopher and poet. In his poem he commented on the various symptoms and signs of syphilis and its treatment. He attributed the origin of the disease to a punishment inflicted by the god Apollo on a poor shepherd named Syphilius, who had angered the god by building altars on a sacred hill. The infected shepherd was advised by the nymph Ammerice, the guardian of the forests, to ask forgiveness of the god. He was finally cured by the intervention of Apollo, who was responsible for providing a treatment for the disease in the form of guaiacum or the 'wood of life' *(lignum vitae)*. It has been called syphilis ever since, a sad tribute to a poor sacrilegious shepherd. Wrote Fracastoro:

He first wore buboes dreadful to the sight
Felt strange pains, and sleepless passed the night.
From him the malady received its name
The neighbouring shepherds catch'd the spreading flame.

The manifestations of the different stages of syphilis were often spectacular and frequently very repulsive, and it

---

*Girolamo Fracastoro (1478-1553), an Italian physician, though steeped in medical traditions of the Middle Ages, preserved some sort of an independent outlook, and in 1546, published a famous text *De Contagione et Contagiosis Morbis* ('On Contagion and Contagious Diseases').

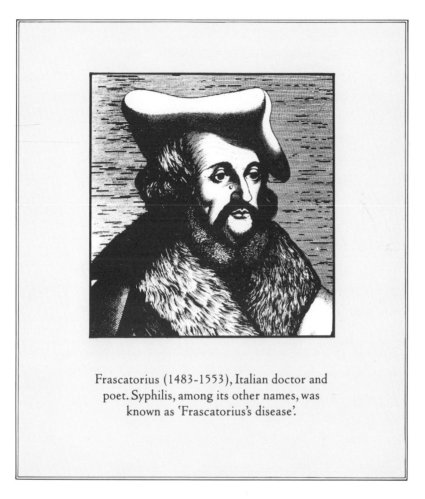

Frascatorius (1483-1553), Italian doctor and poet. Syphilis, among its other names, was known as 'Frascatorius's disease'.

is not surprising that Shakespeare used many word-portraits to emphasise them. He referred to 'the malady of France' in at least seven of his plays, and his observations were accurate and, in some instances, quite elaborate. His references to venereal disease appeared about ninety years after Fracastoro called it the 'French disease'; however, the name

Thersites (Norman Rodway) and Achilles (Alan
Howard), in a production of *Troilus and Cressida* by
the Royal Shakespeare Theatre in 1968.
Photograph from the Tom Holte Theatre
Photographic Collection; courtesy of The
Shakespeare Birthplace Trust.

'syphilis', after Fracastoro's shepherd, was not used till much later. The French, not wishing to have the indignity of such a dread disease named after them, termed it the 'Neapolitan disease', because the French soldiers had returned from Italy with the disease.

Thersites, a deformed and scurrilous Greek, who was noted for his famous comment 'All the argument is a cuckold and a whore', made this reference to the Neapolitan disease (*Troilus and Cressida*, II, iii, 16):

> After this, the vengeance on the whole camp! or, rather, the Neapolitan bone-ache![1] for that, methinks, is the curse depending on those that war for a placket.[2]

In another play, a clown, speaking from experience, enquires from some musicians (*Othello*, III,i,3):

> 'Why masters, ha your instruments been in Naples,[3] that they speak i' the nose[4] thus?'

Shakespeare used an extremely polite term, 'instrument',* to refer to the genital organs, and, in similar vein, 'placket'* was an opening in a skirt or petticoat from whence the disease was often acquired!

---

*instrument, placket: 'instrument', by innuendo, probably meant the penis, and was also mentioned by Hortensio, an amorous man in the disguise of a music teacher, who says to his pupil, Bianca: 'Madam, before you touch the instrument, To learn the order of my fingering, I must begin with rudiments of art' (*Taming of the Shrew*, III, i, 62). Similarly, 'placket', an opening in a petticoat, also has a sexual connotation. Edgar, in disguise, tells King Lear: 'Keep thy foot out of brothels, thy hand out of plackets ... (*Lear*, III, iv, 94). Again, in *The Winter's Tale* (IV, iv, 238): 'Is there no manners left among maids? Will they wear their plackets where they should bear their faces?'

[73]

The 'French crown' has been considered to be syphilitic turbercles, which were apparently a common secondary manifestation. The particular form was also called *le chapelet,* since the tubercles were to be found about the forehead and temples and behind the ears, vaguely in the form of a crown. This French crown is spoken of and associated with another complication of the secondary stages, alopecia:

> *Quince.* Some of your French crowns have no hair at all,[5]
> > *Midsummer Night's Dream,* I, ii, 86

> *Falstaff.* Bardolph was shav'd[6] and lost many a hair ...
> > 1 *King Henry IV,* III, iii, 59

> *Dromio.* Not a man of those but he hath the wit to lose his hair.
> *Antipholus.* Why, thou didst conclude hairy man plain dealers without wit.
> *Dromio.* The plainer dealer, the sooner lost; yet he loseth it in a kind of jollity.[7]
> > *Comedy of Errors,* II, ii, 83

The traditional role of prostitutes in the spread of the disease was well known, and it was commonly associated with loose living. A humble English soldier named Pistol reminisces at the end of a battle with the French (*King Henry V,* V, i, 75):

> News have I that my Nell* is dead i' th' spital[8]
> Of malady of France.

---

*Nell: She was called Doll in some texts. Pistol married Mrs Quickly and not Doll Tearsheet, who was last heard of as being treated in the hospital for venereal diseases *(King Henry V,* II, 1, 72-74).

Poor Pistol, defeated, diseased and downcast, goes on to say that he will return to his country (with a pun on the word 'steal'), become a brothel ('bawd') keeper, patch up his syphilitic sores and make out that he received them in the French wars (V, i, 79):

Honour is cudgell'd, Well, bawd I'll turn,
And something lean to cutpurse of quick hand;
To England will I steal, and there I'll steal;
And patches will I get unto these cudgell'd scars,
And swear I got them in the Gallia wars.

Prostitutes often lived in favoured places. The land and houses in the neighbourhood of the theatre district in London were part of the diocese of the Bishop of Winchester. The brothels of London were situated in this area and were known as the 'Winchester stews', while their occupants were the 'Winchester geese'. So also were the prototypes of two of Shakespeare's characters with very appropriate names, Doll Tearsheet (in 2 *King Henry IV*) and Mistress Overdone *(Measure for Measure)*. The 'Winchester geese', however, were referred to in *Troilus and Cressida,* one of the most puzzling of Shakespeare's plays, and in some ways an unpleasant one. It is not, as with others, the story of the death of a hero, but its theme is lechery and vice. The very last three lines in this play (V, x, 53), spoken by Pandarus, are a sad comment on the spread of venereal disease by the 'Winchester geese':

Some galled[9] goose of Winchester[10] would hiss.
Till then I'll sweat and seek about for eases,
And at that time bequeath you my diseases.

A 16th Century bath establishment. Such
communal baths were eventually banned, as they led
to promiscuity and the spread of venereal disease.
From the book of Johann Stumpff, Zurich, 1548.
(From *A History of Medicine* by A. Castiglioni, 1941.)

The Bishop of Winchester's privilege of having brothels
situated in his diocese is alluded to when the Duke of
Gloucester is quarrelling with the Bishop at the gates of the
Tower of London. Gloucester *(1 King Henry VI, I, iii, 35)*
thus taunts his priestly antagonist: 'Thou that giv'st whores

indulgences to sin.' And again, (I, iii, 53) when rallying his men to fight against the Bishop:

> *Gloucester.* Winchester goose! I cry 'A rope! a rope!'
> Now beat them hence; why do you let them stay?
> Thee I'll chase hence, thou wolf in sheep's array
> Out tawny-coats! Out, scarlet hypocrite!

In the following description, the bone (or bone marrow) would appear to have been affected (*Measure for Measure*, I, ii, 51).

> *1 Gentleman.* Thou art always figuring[11] diseases in me, but thou art full of error; I am sound.
> *Lucio.* Nay, not as one would say, healthy; but so sound as things that are hollow; thy bones are hollow, impiety has made a feast of thee.

It seems from the context of the same conversation, between the first Gentleman and Lucio (I, ii, 56), that arthritic complications were also a problem:

> *1 Gentleman.* How now! which of your hips has the most profound sciatica?

To the other manifestations may be added syphilitic skin lesions, mentioned by the demented Timon (*Timon of Athens*, III, vi, 98):

> Of man and beast the infinite malady
> Crust you quite o'er![12]

Ulcers and sores were some of the dreaded complications of advanced syphilis, and in *As You Like It* (II, vii, 64) are vividly described in the Duke's indictment of Jaques, one of the lords attending on him.

Most mischievous foul sin, in chiding sin;
For thou thyself hast been a libertine,
As sensual as the brutish sting[13] itself;
And all th' embossed sores and headed evils
That thou with license of free foot [14] has caught
Would'st thou disgorge into the general world.

And again, the unpleasant appearance of syphilitic ulcers is described by the demented Timon (IV, iii, 39):

She whom the spital-house[15] and ulcerous sores
Would cast the gorge[16] at ...

The grave-digger in *Hamlet* must have buried many a person whom he believed to have died from 'the pox', as evidenced by the remarks of one of the clowns in the grave-digging scene (V, i, 158):

Hamlet. How long will a man be i' th' earth ere he rot?
1 Clown. Faith, if 'a be not rotten before 'a die – as we have many pocky corses now-a-days that will scarce hold the laying in – a' will last you some eight year or nine year. A tanner will last you nine year.

An old English term for venereal sores is used by King Lear when trying to console Cordelia (*Lear*, V, iii, 23):

Lear. 			Wipe thine eyes
The good years* shall devour them, flesh and fell
Ere they shall make us weep.

The spread of the disease from prostitutes, and such

---

*In earlier editions 'good years' appeared as 'goujeers'. The phrase 'what the goodyear' meant 'what the deuce'; hence 'goodyear' means something vaguely evil.

Timon (Paul Scofield) and Flavius (Tony Church), from Act IV, Scene III,
of a production of *Timon of Athens* by the Royal Shakespeare Theatre
in 1965. Photograph by Gordon Goode; reproduced by courtesy
of The Shakespeare Birthplace Trust, Shakespeare Centre Library.

limited treatment as was available, are briefly described in
two plays:

> *Pistol.* No; to the spital[17] go,
> And from the powd'ring tub[18] of infamy
> Fetch forth the lazar kite[19] of Cressid's kind,[20]
> Doll Tearsheet she by name, and her espouse.
>
> *King Henry V,* II, i, 72

[79]

Timon. Be a whore still; they love thee not that use thee.
Give them diseases, leaving with thee their lust.
Make use of thy salt[21] hours. Season[22] the slaves
For tubs and baths;[23] bring down rose-cheek'd youth
To the tub-fast[24] and the diet.

Timon of Athens, IV, ii, 83

Syphilis was evidently very prevalent and widespread. Sergeant-Surgeon William Clowes, in 1585, wrote *A Brief and Necessary Treatise Touching the Cure of the Disease Called Morbus Gallicus or Lues Venera, by Unctions etc.*, in which he presented startling facts and figures regarding its incidence in London. He reports:

> It happened in the House of Sir Bartholomew whilst I served there for the space of 9-10 years, that among every twenty diseased persons that were taken in, ten of them had the pockes ... I may speak boldly because I speak truly, and yet I speak it with very grief of heart, that in the hospital of St Bartholomew in London there have been cured of this disease by me and three others within the space of five years to the number of one thousand and more. I speak nothing of St Thomas' hospital and other houses in the City wherein an infinite number are daily in cure.

The population of London at this time was about 124 000, which would have easily put syphilis amongst the commonest of diseases. So much for the permissive society of those days!

The available treatment of syphilis was by this time probably known in a vague sort of a way to most sufferers. The 'tub-fast' and 'diet' referred to the accepted means of treatment. The 'powdering tub of infamy' was, in fact, a tub in

Mercury fumigation ('the powd'ring tub of infamy',
King Henry V) was used in the treatment of
syphilitic patients. The secondary and tertiary
stages are depicted here. (From Steven Blankaart,
Die belagert und entsetzte Venus, 1689, in the National
Library of Medicine, Bethesda.)

which the patient was exposed to the fumes from the powder of cinnabar, an ore of mercury. This was thrown on a hot-plate, and as it volatilised and condensed it settled as a powder on the patient's body.

Ambroise Paré* records the treatment of syphilis as follows:

> Some have devised a fourth manner of curing the 'lues venera', which is suffitus or fumigatus. They put the patient under a tent or canopy made close on every side, lest anything should expire, and they put in unto him a vessel with hot coals, whereupon they plentifully throw cinnabaris, so that they may on every side enjoy the rising fume.

Paré also described 'a barrel fitted to reserve the fumes in':

> You may put the patient naked into the barrel, so that he may sit on a seat or board perforated, thus the patient shall easily receive the fume that exhales and none of it be lost, he covering and venting himself on every side.

'Sweating-houses' and 'tubs' were still in existence in London in the time of Charles I, and were located in Leather Lane in Holborn. Again, with reference to the 'tub' (*Measure for Measure*, III, ii.50):

> *Lucio.* How doth my dear morsel, thy mistress?
> Procures she still, ha?

---

*Ambroise Paré (1510-90), a Frenchman, began his career as an apprentice to a barber-surgeon. He then served for some years as an assistant surgeon on the *Hôtel-Dieu*, a famous Paris hospital. After several years on active service as an army surgeon he became the foremost surgeon in France.

Pompey. Troth, sir, she hath eaten up all her beef, and she is herself in the tub.

Mercury had been used in the treatment of leprosy since the twelfth century, when this disease was brought back from Palestine by the Crusaders. It was used as an ointment called Saracen's ointment and, not surprisingly, was ineffective in curing this disease. As the manifestations of late or advanced syphilis resembled those of leprosy, mercury was introduced in the 1400s for the treatment of syphilis. Centuries later it was still the mainstay of treatment until Paul Ehrlich, in 1911, discovered his 'magic bullet', salvarsan or '606', which contained arsenic.

A vivid clinical picture is described when the demented Timon advises two rapacious courtesans to take their revenge on men, including, as it does, a list of the tertiary effects of the venereal spirochaete infection. No doubt Shakespeare recorded what was in his day a common enough sight – fortunately, rare today! (*Timon*, IV, iii, 150):

> Consumption sow
> In hollow bones of man; strike their sharp shins,
> And mar men's spurring.[25] Crack the lawyer's voice,
> That he may never more false title plead,
> Nor sound his quillets[26] shrilly. Hoar[27] the flamen,[28]
> That scolds against the quality[29] of flesh,
> And not believes himself. Down with the nose,[30]
> Down with it flat, take the bridge quite away
> Of him that, his particular to foresee,
> Smells from the general weal.[31] Make curl'd-pate ruffians
> bald,
> And let the unscarr'd braggarts[32] of the war

[83]

A Spanish soldier suffering from 'Neapolitan Disease' (syphilis), later known as 'French disease', under 'tub' treatment with mercury fumes. His clothes are being treated too. Reproduced by courtesy of the World Health Organization, Geneva.

Derive some pain from you. Plague all,
That your activity may defeat and quell
The source of all erection.

This is one of Shakespeare's most classic descriptions of a single disease. Bucknill, in 1860, wrote:

Among all these symptoms of 'the malady of France', the only ambiguous one is the first, in which the word 'consumption' seems to be somewhat indefinitely applied. It seems most probable that consumptions in the hollow bones means disease of the bones of the cranium which form that which may essentially be called the 'hollow bone of the body'.

Diseases of the cranial and other bones have been common since ancient times, and have given the clinical picture of cranial tabes. Painful nodes on the shin bones (periostitis) are probably meant by the expression 'strike their sharp shins'. Venereal ulceration of the larynx is next referred to – 'crack the lawyer's voice …'. The cleric (flamen) is made to bear the mark of infamy in the form of the white scaly skin eruption, probably a psoriatic syphilide. The next symptoms apply to that hideous disfigurement of chronic syphilis, loss of the nasal bones – 'take the bridge away'. The fearful list of the effects of the chronic syphilis is concluded by impotence and baldness; the former is especially remarkable, as it was not observed to be a symptom of the disease until shortly before Shakespeare wrote this play.

Woodcut Entitled 'Impatience' from a
Netherlands *ars moriendi* (the art of dying), c. 1450.
A dying man, tempted by the devil, kicks the doctor
and his attendants away from his bedside.
Reproduced by courtesy of the British Library, London.

5
SHAKESPEARE'S EPILEPTICS

HE 'SACRED DISEASE', an ancient name for epilepsy, is probably one of the oldest disorders known to man. It was written up by both the ancient Egyptians and the Hebrews; but Hippocrates, about 400 B.C., said: 'The sacred disease appears to me to be no more divine, no more sacred than other diseases …' One would say of an epileptic fit that it had 'seized' a man. This description was probably derived from the belief that fits were considered visitations by gods or demons, and accounted for the name the 'sacred disease'. Most sixteenth and seventeenth century physicians believed that epileptic attacks were linked to demoniac possession. Few doubted the existence of Satan, and it was a common practice to consider that a man suffering from fits was possessed. If a physician was called in, he applied the standard treatment for the 'falling sickness' in the form of enemas, purges, cuppings, sweatings, and so on. If these failed to produce results, a malign influence was at work. 'A plague upon your epileptic visage!' is a curse which Kent calls down on the despised Oswald in *King Lear*. The startling appearance of the symptoms and the belief that epilepsy was incurable must have contributed to its reputation.

Some of Shakespeare's most prominent characters were epileptics. He introduced epilepsy as an illness suffered by Julius Caesar, Othello and Macbeth – a remarkable trio of epileptics, considering that these were leading characters from his best-known tragedies. With no treatment available to control the fits, there would have been many opportunities for the playwright to observe and describe the rather startling clinical features of an epileptic seizure. Moreover, he used this illness to heighten the dramatic effect of the play on the audience.

Consider Julius Caesar, for example, whose life was cut short by his Senators. When they planned his murder, they considered his physical attributes, among them, his epilepsy. Cassius tells Brutus (*Julius Caesar*, I, ii, 120):

> And when the fit was on him I did mark
> How he did shake. 'Tis true, this god did shake.

Later, Casca describes how Caesar was offered the crown by the people, and he refused it; during the commotion 'he swooned' and had an epileptic seizure (I, ii, 243);

> *Casca.* And then he offered it the third time; he put it the third time by; and still as he refus'd it ... for he swooned and fell down at it ...
> *Cassius.* But soft, I pray you. What, did Caesar swoon?
> *Casca.* He fell down in the market-place, and foam'd at the mouth, and was speechless.
> *Brutus.* 'Tis very like. He hath the falling sickness ...[1]
> *Casca.* I know not what you mean by that, but I am sure Caesar fell down ...
> *Brutus.* What said he when he came unto himself?

Uroscopy. Because of the emphasis placed on examining urine, the urine flask was to some extent the symbol of the physician. The urine's colour, sediment, smell, consistency and, possibly, taste, helped to diagnose what was wrong with the patient, predict his prognosis, and provide guidance as to treatment. (From Biblioteca de la Facultad de Medicina, Madrid.)

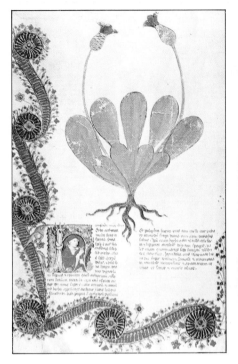

Above: The mandrake root is mentioned more often than any other plant in Shakespeare's plays. This beautiful illustration of the root is a typical mediaeval botanical illustration, more artistic than real. (From *Historia Plantarum,* by courtesy of Biblioteca Casanatense, Rome.)

Right: A Painting from Avicenna's Cannon. He is giving directions for the preparation of drugs at an apothecary's shop. (Courtesy of Biblioteca Universitaria di Bologna, MS 2197.)

'The Doctor's Visit' by Franz van Mieris the Elder.
Feeling the pulse had been part of clinical
examination since Galen, but it was not until the
invention of the minute hand in watches that the
rate could be accurately counted. (Courtesy of
Kunsthistorisches Museum, Vienna.)

Casca. Marry, before he fell down, when he perceiv'd the
common herd was glad he refus'd the crown, he pluckt me ope
his doublet,[2] and offer'd them his throat to cut ...
And so he fell. When he came to himself again, he said, if he
had done or said anything amiss, he desir'd their worships to
think it was his infirmity.

Caesar's fit does not actually take place on the stage, but is
described by other characters in the play. In *Othello*. however,
the fit takes place on the stage. The pre-epileptic aura immediately preceding the fit, in this case Othello's mental
confusion and senseless muttering, is demonstrated (IV, i, 35):

Othello. Lie with her – lie on her? We say lie on her when they
belie her. Lie with her.
Zounds, that's fulsome. Handkerchief – confessions –
handkerchief! To confess, and be hang'd for his labour – first, to
be hang'd, and then to confess. I tremble at it. Nature would not
invest herself in such shadowing passion without some
instruction. It is not words that shakes me thus – pish! noses,
ears, and lips. Is't possible?
Confess! – handkerchief! O devil! [*falls in a trance*]
Iago. Work on, my medicine, work ...
Cassio. What's the matter?
Iago.
My lord is fall'n into an epilepsy.
This is his second fit; he had one yesterday.
Cassio. Rub him about the temples.
Iago.   No, forbear.
The lethargy[3] must have his quiet course;
If not, he foams at mouth, and by and by
Breaks out to savage madness. Look, he stirs.
Do you withdraw yourself a little while;
He will recover straight ...

Othello's epileptic fit appeared when he was finally convinced of his wife's unfaithfulness. At that particular moment in the play the sympathy of the audience is transferred to Othello, and the epileptic attack serves to increase the drama of the impending tragedy.

Macbeth is a play with a villain as a hero. Lady Macbeth, as evil as her husband, and an expert at planning murders, hires men to kill her husband's opponents. They report to Macbeth at a banquet that Banquo is dead; but when he learns that Banquo's son escaped the murderers, the anxiety of the whole situation brings on a seizure (III, iv, 21):

> *Macbeth.* Then comes my fit again. I had else been perfect,
> Whole as the marble, founded as the rock,
> As broad and general as the casing[4] air,
> But now I am cabin'd, cribb'd,[5] confin'd, bound in
> To saucy[6] doubts and fears.

Lady Macbeth then reassures her guests that her husband's fit is short-lived, that he will be better soon, and asks them not to panic (III, iv, 52):

> *Lady Macbeth.* Sit, worthy friends. My lord is often thus,
> And hath been from his youth. Pray you, keep seat.
> The fit is momentary; upon a thought[7]
> He will again be well. If much you note him,
> You shall offend him and extend his passion.[8]
> Feed, and regard him not.

The life of King Henry IV spanned three plays, and his death, which was preceded by a fit, was recorded in Part 2 of *King Henry IV*. A fit, the 'falling sickness', apoplexy and

Cassio (Basil Hoskins), Iago (Emlyn Williams),
and Othello (Harry Andrews), in Act IV, Scene I,
of a production of *Othello* by the Shakespeare
Memorial Theatre in 1956. Photograph by Angus
McBean; reproduced by courtesy of The
Shakespeare Birthplace Trust.

epilepsy were a loosely defined group of symptoms, with no clear demarcation between them. Warwick referred to King Henry's terminal illness as a 'fit'. In his deathbed scene King Henry is surrounded by his sons, Prince Hal, Gloucester (Prince Humphrey) and Clarence, as well as the Earls of Westmoreland and Warwick. The King falls into a 'fit', and this is discussed by the Princes. He recovers sufficiently to question his eldest son, Prince Henry, whom he suspects of wishing to steal his crown. As his illness comes on, he speaks as follows (2 *King Henry IV,* IV, iv, 110; IV, v, 1):

> *King.* And now my sight fails, and my brain is giddy.
> O me! come near me now I am much ill.
> *Prince Humphrey.* Comfort, your Majesty!
>
> ...
>
> *Westmoreland.* My sovereign lord, cheer up yourself, look up.
> *Warwick.* Be patient, Princes; you do not know these fits
> Are with his Highness very ordinary.
> Stand from him, give him air; he'll straight⁹ be well.
> *Clarence.* No, no; he cannot long hold out these pangs.
> Th' incessant care and labour of his mind
> Hath wrought the mure¹⁰ that should confine it in
> So thin that life looks through and will break out.
>
> ...
>
> *Warwick.* Speak lower,¹¹ Princes, for the King recovers.
> *Prince Humphrey.* This apoplexy will certain be his end.

At this point King Henry pulls himself together sufficiently to ask to be carried to another room in the palace:

> *King.* I pray you, take me up, and bear me hence
> Into some other chamber. Softly, pray.

Let there be no noise made, my gentle friends;
Unless some dull and favourable[12] hand
Will whisper music to my weary spirit.

...

Clarence. His eye is hollow, and he changes[13] much.
Warwick. Less noise, less noise!
Prince Henry. If he be sick with joy, he'll recover without physic.

...

Warwick. Not so much noise, my lords. Sweet Prince, speak low
The King your father is disposed to sleep.

The history of the treatment of epilepsy, as of many other diseases, unfortunately showed a great variety of irrational manoeuvres. The mediaeval physicians' regimen of drugs, cauterisation and trephining followed ancient traditions. In the eighteenth century, Tissot* saw trephining as a treatment for contusion of the skull or head injuries. He was also interested in epilepsy and was a keen observer of the disease. He recognised that the predisposing causes of epilepsy were not known, but advocated that the patient be kept on a healthy regime and free from excitement. The exact steps were decided for each individual. In short, this was the treatment of the epileptic patient rather than the disease – which perhaps is the key to the practice of good medicine.

---

*Tissot (1728-97), a Swiss physician, in 1770 published in French a 'Treatise on Epilepsy', in which he distinguished between *grand mal* and *petit mal*. Tissot reported the case of a fourteen-year-old girl in his 'Treatise'. Her attacks went on for many years, and 'during part of this time the young patient, in the intervals between the great attacks (*grands accès*), frequently had very short, little (*petits*) attacks, which were merely marked by an instantaneous loss of consciousness interrupting her speech, together with a very slight movement of the eyes. Often, when recovering, she finished the sentence in the middle of which she had been interrupted ...'

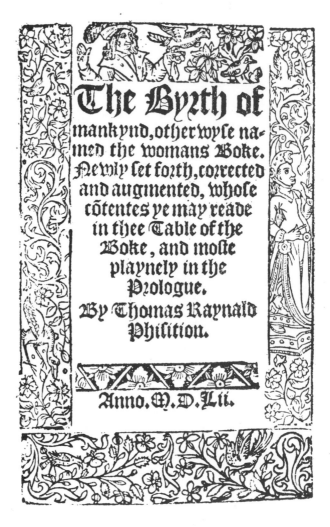

Title page of *The Byrth of mankynd, otherwyse named the womans Boke*, 1552 edition, by E. Roeslin the Elder; a popular textbook of midwifery with a very appropriate title. (From *A Catalogue of Sixteenth Century Medical Books in Edinburgh Libraries*, compiled by D. T. Bird, 1982; courtesy of the Royal College of Physicians of Edinburgh.)

6
PREGNANCY
&
CHILDBIRTH

Lear. Thou knows't the first time that we smell the air
We wawl and cry.
                    King Lear, IV, vi, 179

HE PRACTICE OF MIDWIFERY is probably the most ancient branch of medicine. From time immemorial a woman in labour has received some sort of assistance from another person. Abnormality and danger have always been recognised as ever-present possibilities, and hence rules and regulations, the tradition of the lying-in chamber, have been evolved and formulated in some far-distant abyss of time, and handed down from one woman to another throughout the long course of the ages. Even at the present day, as every *accoucheur* knows, the tedium of waiting is relieved by the circulation of advice and warnings, good, bad and indifferent. It was in the wake of these traditions that the art and science of midwifery took shape. No wonder, therefore, that the familiar and recurring miracle of childbirth, from conception to the onset of labour and delivery, was the subject of many comments in Shakespeare's plays. The secret hope of every parent that a normal child will be born without any blemish or congenital defect is ex-

[95]

pressed by Oberon, the King of the Fairies, in the fantasy
world of *A Midsummer Night's Dream* (V, i, 398):

> And the blots of Nature's hand
> Shall not in their issue stand;
> Never mole, hare-lip, nor scar,
> Nor mark prodigious,[1] such as are
> Despised in nativity,
> Shall upon their children be.

There was a general belief in those mediaeval days that
the effects of many diseases and their consequences were
transmitted by the parents to the unborn child. This fear is
expressed by an unusual character, Launcelot Gobbo, Shylock's servant. He is not happy with Shylock's intention to
obtain his 'pound of flesh' and fears the consequences *(Merchant of Venice*, III, v,1):

> Yes, truly; for, look you, the sins of the
> father are to be laid upon the children ...

The days of effective contraception were centuries away,
and it was not uncommon for another pregnancy to occur
before a woman had recovered from the effects of the previous one. Leontes, King of Sicilia, openly accuses his wife,
Hermione, of having a bastard child by Polixenes, King of
Bohemia. In her defence she brings up this possibility *(The
Winter's Tale*, III, ii, 100):

> with immodest hatred
> The child-bed privilege denied,[2] which 'longs[3]
> To women of all fashion ...

Identical twins, who arrived on the heels of a previous

pregnancy, are the basis of the confusion in *The Comedy of Errors* (I, i, 50):

Ægeon. There had she not been long but she became
A joyful mother of two goodly sons;
And, which was strange, the one so like the other
As could not be distinguish'd but by names.

The moment of conception is described in a rather fundamental manner in *Measure for Measure* (I, iv, 40):

Lucio. Your brother and his lover have embrac'd.
As those that feed grow full, as blossoming time
That from the seedness[4] the bare fallow brings
To teeming foison,[5] even so her plenteous womb
Expresseth his full tilth and husbandry.

It is also described in a rather blunt statement using Hymen, the god of marriage, as the natural cause *(Pericles,* III, i, 9):

Gower. Hymen* hath brought the bride to bed,
Where, by the loss of maidenhead,
A babe is moulded.[6]

The age of consent and the legal marriageable age were not controlled by law, but were often dependent on parents' wishes; hence early betrothals and marriages were common. In *Romeo and Juliet* the argument is over Juliet's marriage,

---

*Hymen was at first the name of a marriage song among the Greeks. Later it became the name of the god of marriage, and Hymen was supposed to be the son of Apollo and one of the Muses. Wedding guests made sacrifices to him for the happiness of the bride and groom.

and expresses the divergent views of Capulet (Juliet's father), Lady Capulet (her mother) and Paris (whom Juliet was supposed to marry before Romeo came on the scene). Juliet was only fourteen years of age. Capulet was eventually justified in his plea for a postponement of the marriage, as subsequent events proved (I, ii, 8):

> *Capulet.* My child is yet a stranger in the world,
> She hath not seen the change of fourteen years;
> Let two more summers wither in their pride
> Ere we may think her ripe to be a bride.
> *Paris.* Younger than she are happy mothers made.
> *Capulet.* And too soon marr'd are those so early made.

Lady Capulet eventually relents, and in the next scene she tells Juliet (I, iii, 70):

> *Lady Capulet.* Well, think of marriage now.
> Younger than you ... ladies of esteem
> Are made already mothers. By my count
> I was your mother much upon these years
> That you are now a maid.

Some of the signs and symptoms of pregnancy are described with remarkable use of unusual words *(Love's Labour's Lost,* V, ii, 665):

> *Costard.* ... the poor wench is cast away. She's quick; the child brags in her belly already.

A better description of a pregnant woman would be hard to find than this *(Winter's Tale,* II, i, 19):

> *2 Lady.*   She is spread of late
> Into a goodly bulk. Good time encounter her![7]

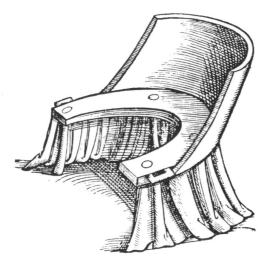

The birthing chair: a convenient apparatus for use
in childbirth, on which a woman may rest comfortably
and, surrounded by her attendants, give birth in a
semi-seated position. (From Rueff's *De conceptu
et generatione hominis*, 1554; courtesy of the
New York Academy of Medicine Library.)

Of the more advanced state of pregnancy, Shakespeare
makes an observation, perhaps a trifle exaggerated, about
the effects of such big-bellied women in a crowd. The crowd
in this case is part of the pageantry at the coronation of
Queen Anne, and the statements are made by three 'gentlemen' in a street at Westminster (*King Henry VIII*, IV, i, 76):

> Great-bellied women,[8]
> That had not half a week to go, like rams[9]
> In the old time of war, would shake the press,[10]
> And make 'em reel before 'em.

In addition to his reference to 'big-bellied' women, Shakespeare went a step further to describe the 'swimming gait' of a woman in the advanced stages of pregnancy. Titania, the Queen of the Fairies, tells her King (*Midsummer Night's Dream*, II, i, 129):

> And grow big-bellied with the wanton wind;
> Which she, with pretty and with swimming gait
> Following – her womb then rich with my young squire.

The 'joys' of pregnancy are summed up by Ægeon, a merchant of Syracuse (*Comedy of Errors*, I, i, 47): 'The pleasing punishment that women bear ...'

During pregnancy some women have 'cravings',* or abnormal and compelling longings for unusual types of food. This state is described in the rather unusual story which Pompey tells the Magistrate in *Measure for Measure* (II, i, 86-95):

> Sir, she came in great with child; and longing,
> saving your honour's reverence,[11] for stew'd prunes ...
> being, as I say, with child, and being
> great-bellied, and longing, as I said, for prunes ...

Again, the cravings of a pregnant woman are referred to in *Troilus and Cressida* (III, iii, 237):

> I have a woman's longing
> An appetite that I am sick withal.

A folk-lore belief was that a woman's thoughts could have

---

*This kind of perverted appetite, known as pica, is from the Latin for a magpie.

an influence on her pregnancy, on the child, and even on the manner of delivery. During the child-bearing period demonic beings were considered particularly harmful, as superstitious people believed in these things and accepted their implication without question. The birth of Gloucester is described as ill-omened and difficult (3 *King Henry VI*, V, vi, 49):

> *King Henry.* Thy mother felt more than a mother's pain,
> And yet brought forth less than a mother's hope,
> To wit, an indigest and deformed lump,
> Not like the fruit of such a goodly tree.
> Teeth hadst thou in thy head when thou wast born,
> To signify thou cam'st to bite the world.

Later in the same scene, Gloucester relates that his birth was a footling presentation and that he was born with teeth (V, vi, 70):

> For I have often heard my mother say
> I came into the world with my legs forward.[12]
> Had I not reason, think ye, to make haste
> And seek their ruin that usurp'd our right?
> The midwife wondered; and the women cried,
> 'O, Jesus bless us, he is born with teeth!'
> And so I was, which plainly signified
> That I should snarl, and bite, and play the dog.
> Then, since the heavens have shap'd my body so,
> Let hell make crook'd my mind to answer it.

In *King Richard III* he speaks as follows (I, i, 18):

> I – that am curtail'd[13] of this fair proportion,[14]
> Cheated of feature by dissembling[15] nature,
> Deformed, unfinish'd, sent before my time

> Into this breathing world scarce half made up,
> And that so lamely and unfashionable
> That dogs bark at me as I halt[16] by them …

Somewhere in the foregoing two quotations can be read the tragic possibility of giving birth to a child with congenital defects. The belief in maternal impression as the cause of congenital abnormalities and deformities was widespread. For this reason, the mother was expected to protect herself from things that terrified her, such as fire, thunder and lightning, and from the sight of deformed humans and animals, as all of these could lead to birth deformities. It was also thought that the moon in some way was responsible for congenital deformities, which is probably why Caliban, a deformed monster, is called 'Mooncalf' by Stephano. King Lear in his madness brought in sterility as a curse and then elaborated even further (I, iv, 278):

> Into her womb convey sterility;
> Dry up in her the organs of increase;[17]
> And from her derogate[18] body never spring
> A babe to honour her! If she must teem[19]
> Create her child of spleen,[20] that it may live
> And be a thwart disnatur'd[21] torment to her.
> Let it stamp wrinkles in her brow of youth,
> With cadent[22] tears fret[23] channels in her cheeks,
> Turn all her mother's pains and benefits
> To laughter and contempt, that she may feel
> How sharper than a serpent's tooth it is
> To have a thankless child!

Also, in *King Richard II*, we read (II, ii, 64):

> *Queen.* Now hath my soul brought forth her prodigy;[24]

And I, a gasping new-deliver'd mother,
Have woe to woe, sorrow to sorrow, join'd.

And in *The Tempest* (I, ii, 120):

Miranda. Good wombs have borne bad sons.

A protection from sterility is spoken of by Plutarch, who refers to the remarkable feast of Lupercalia, an ancient Roman festival, in which noble young men run naked through the streets of the Palatine precinct, striking in sport anyone who comes in their way with leather thongs. A woman so struck was made fertile and could look forward to bearing her child early. This is mentioned in *Julius Caesar* (I, ii, 3):

Caesar. Calphurnia.
Calphurnia. Here, my lord.
Caesar. Stand you directly in Antonius' way
When he doth run his course. Antonius!
Antonius. Caesar, my lord.
Caesar. Forget not, in your speed, Antonius,
To touch Calphurnia; for our elders say,
The barren, touched in this holy chase,
Shake off their sterile curse.

The death of a foetus, or its macerated retention in the uterus, probably due to syphilis, is put forward by Henry VIII as an excuse for his divorce from Katharine of Aragon (II, iv, 187):

King.   ... who had
Commanded nature that my lady's womb,
If it conceiv'd a male child by me, should
Do no more offices of life to't than
The grave does to the dead; for her male issue

[103]

Alec Clunes as Caliban, in a production of *The
Tempest* by the Shakespeare Memorial Theatre in
1957. Photograph by Angus McBean; courtesy of
The Shakespeare Birthplace Trust.

Or died where they were made, or shortly after
This world had air'd them.

The effect of syphilis on the unborn child was by now beginning to appear in Elizabethan literature. Shakespeare
touched on it in *King Henry VIII,* but the suggestion that the
real King Henry VIII suffered from syphilis is based on the
obstetric history of his first two wives. Henry was aged
eighteen and Katharine of Aragon twenty-four when they
were married in 1509. A year later she was delivered of a
stillborn daughter; a son born in the following year lived
only two months; a third child, born two years later, soon
died; there was another premature delivery in the next year;
and finally, a daughter, Princess Mary, born seven years after
their marriage, lived. Two years later another daughter was
born, only to die in a few months. After 24 years of marriage, Henry VIII divorced Katharine and married Anne
Boleyn (in Shakespeare she was 'Anne Bullen'). The future
Queen Elizabeth was born in 1533. Then followed a miscarriage, and a year later a dead boy was delivered prematurely.
The occurrence of nine pregnancies in two wives with only
two surviving children is strong presumptive evidence of
syphilis. Henry's 'sore legge', which was treated by Thomas
Vicary,* was probably gummatous. It is not surprising that
the unfortunate Mary had a large projecting forehead, thin

---

*The Barber-Surgeons' Company received their charter in 1540 under the
Mastership of the great surgeon Thomas Vicary.

[105]

patchy hair, poorly developed breasts and a grating voice –
stigmata of congenital syphilis. The agony of poor Anne
Bullen at the birth of the future Queen Elizabeth of England
is described (V, i, 18):

> *Lovell.*　　　　　　　　The Queen's in labour,
> They say in great extremity, and fear'd
> She'll with the labour end.

Priapus was the god of copulation, and he was called
upon to produce sterility (*Pericles*, IV, vi, 3): '... freeze the
God Priapus, and undo a whole generation.'

The pains of labour and childbirth are briefly but frequently referred to by Shakespeare:

> *Gower.*　　　　　　　Lucina,†0
> Divinest patroness, and midwife gentle
> To those that cry by night, convey thy deity
> ... make swift the pangs ...
>
> *Pericles*, III, i, 10

> *Aaron.*And from your womb where you imprisoned were
> He is enfranchised[25] and come to light.
>
> *Titus Andronicus*, IV, ii, 124

> *Pauline.*This child was prisoner to the womb, and is
> By law[26] and process of great Nature thence
> Freed and enfranchis'd ...
>
> *Winter's Tale*, II, ii, 59

---

†Lucina: the Roman goddess of childbirth, a powerful deity who protected Roman
women in labour.

'Childbirth', by Jost Amman (1580). A birthing
chair is being used, and the baby's horoscope is
being cast at the window. Reproduced from
Medicine and the Artist (Ars Medica) by permission of
the Philadelphia Museum of Art; Dover
Publications, Inc., New York.

The following is partly medical and partly legal, and expresses a merciful aspect of English legal practice: that an unborn child is innocent of the guilt of its mother. A woman condemned to death could plead that she was pregnant. If her plea was accepted, her life was spared until the child was born. When Joan of Arc was condemned to the stake as a sorceress, she claimed a reprieve on these grounds (1 *King Henry VI,* V, iv, 59):

> Will nothing turn your unrelenting hearts?
> Then, Joan, discover thine infirmity,
> That warranteth by law to be thy privilege;
> I am with child, ye bloody homicides;
> Murder not then the fruit within my womb,
> Although ye hale me to a violent death.

Delivery by caesarean section is one of the oldest operations in surgery, even if we limit our meaning to its practice during the life of the mother. Its mystical overtones are mentioned in the well-known lines from *Macbeth.* The Thane of Glamis boasts (V, viii, 12):

> *Macbeth.* I bear a charmed life, which must not yield
> To one of woman born.

To which Macduff replies:

> *Macduff.* Despair thy charm;
> And let the angel whom thou still hast serv'd
> Tell thee Macduff was from his mother's womb
> Untimely ripp'd.[27]

Post-mortem caesarean section crops up again in *Cymbe-*

line, with a play upon the name of a man called Posthumus (I, i, 36):

1 *Gentleman.*

for which their father,
Then old and fond of issue, took such sorrow
That he quit being; and his gentle lady,
Big of this gentleman, our theme, deceas'd
As he was born. The King he takes the babe
To his protection, calls him Posthumus Leonatus.

And again in *Cymbeline* (V, iv, 43):

Mother. Lucina lent not me her aid,
But took me in my throes,
That from me was Posthumus ripp'd
Came crying 'mongst his foes,
A thing of pity.

The problem of determination of sex has exercised the ingenuity of medicine-men, philosophers and scientists down the ages, with a result that many theories have been proposed to explain it, and many devices for the purpose of procuring boys or girls according to desire, based upon these theories, have been suggested and tried out. The preference for males still persists strongly in some societies, especially for the first-born. Macbeth wanted nothing but male children and told his wife his feelings (I, vii, 72):

Macbeth. Bring forth men-children only;
For thy undaunted mettle[28] should compose
Nothing but males.

And as a comment for those who have girls, in *The Winter's Tale* (II, ii, 25) we read:

Emilia. She is, something[29] before her time, deliver'd.

Paulina. A boy?
Emilia. A daughter, and a goodly babe,
Lusty, and like to live.

In olden days, and even among uncivilized societies, a parturient woman was seldom or never left to her own resources. While some amateur, such as a grandmother or another woman who had borne children, was sometimes deemed sufficient, nevertheless in most circumstances a 'professional' midwife or 'wise woman' would also be in attendance. The Latin *cum mater* is analogous to the English 'mid-wife' or 'with woman'. Even though relics, charms and incantations were her stock-in-trade, nevertheless the midwife was often considered a woman of great wordly experience and knowledgeable on many subjects (2 *King Henry IV,* II, ii, 26):

> *Prince Henry.* ... the midwives say the children are not in the fault; whereupon the world increases, and kindreds are mightily strengthened.

The Byrth of Mankynde, published in 1540, was the first printed book on midwifery in English, and was the standard guide for midwives and the practice of midwifery for nearly three centuries. It was translated into English by Dr Thomas Raynalde, and the author's intention was clear:

> It is nowe so plainly set forth that the simplest Mydwyfe which can read may both understand for her better instruction and also with other women that have neede of her helpe.

The midwife exhibited a trait perhaps not altogether lacking today — loquacity. In *Titus Andronicus* the nurse was a 'long-tongu'd babbling gossip' (IV, ii, 151) and was mur-

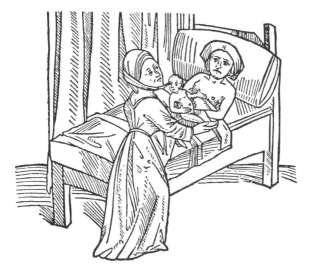

The midwife attending at childbirth, from
Lichtenberger's *Prognosticatio*, Heidelberg, 1488. In
this field of medicine throughout history, women
were always welcome, and even preferred. (From *A
History of Medicine* by A. Castiglioni, 1941.)

dered in order to hide the illegitimacy of her patient!
However, in *Romeo and Juliet*, even though a midwife is called
a 'hag', she is nonetheless praised for her help (I, iv, 92):

> *Mercutio.* This is the hag, when maids lie on their backs,
> That presses them and learns them first to bear,
> Making them women of good carriage.

The birth of an illegitimate child is also the subject of
comment. The Earl of Gloucester admits to Kent that his
son Edmond was a 'bastard son' (*Lear*, I, i, 12, 20):

> Sir, this young fellow's mother could; whereupon she grew

round-womb'd, and had indeed, sir, a son for her cradle ere she had a husband for her bed.

...

Though this knave came something saucily to the world before he was sent for, yet was his mother fair; there was good sport at his making, and the whoreson must be acknowledged.

King John bluntly puts it to one of his nobles, admitting that his brother is a bastard (*King John*, I, i, 117):

Your father's wife did after wedlock bear him,
And if she did play false, the fault was hers;
Which fault lies on the hazards of all husbands
That marry wives.

King John's bastard brother was unfortunately fourteen weeks premature (I, i, 109):

Upon his death-bed he by will bequeath'd
His lands to me, and took it on his death[30]
That this my mother's son was none of his;
And if he were, he came into the world
Full fourteen weeks before the course of time.

Edgar and Edmund, sons of the Earl of Gloucester, are in opposite camps, Edmund being a 'bastard son to Gloucester'. Edgar speaks (*King Lear*, V, iii, 170):

Edgar. The gods are just, and of our pleasant vices
Make intruments to plague us ...

This does not refer to venereal disease, but to the illegitimate birth of Edmund, although it is frequently used as a quotation applicable to diseases arising from vicious habits. A miscarriage was a cause for regret (*Love's Labour's Lost*, I, i, 104):

Biron. Why should I joy in any abortive birth?

The birth of twins was invariably a special occasion, an unusual natural phenomenon (*Timon*, IV, iii, 3):

Timon.   Twinn'd brothers of one womb
Whose procreation, residence, and birth
Scarce is dividant ...[31]

And (*Comedy of Errors*, V, i, 424):

We came into the world like brother and brother,
And now let's go hand in hand, not one before another.

The contentment of a nursing mother is expressed by Cleopatra (*Antony and Cleopatra*, V, ii, 306):

Peace, peace!
Dost thou not see my baby at my breast
That sucks the nurse asleep?

On lactation, Lady Macbeth expresses a maternal instinct, rather unusual for her (I, vii, 54):

I have given suck, and know
How tender 'tis to love the babe that milks me.

The eagerly awaited first cry of a newborn baby to signify his presence in the world cannot be better described than in the words of Lear (IV, vi, 183):

When we are born, we cry that we are come
To this great stage of fools.

Falstaff (Anthony Quayle) and Bardolph (Michael
Bates), in a production of *King Henry IV* by the
Shakespeare Memorial Theatre in 1951.
Photograph by Angus McBean; reproduced by
courtesy of The Shakespeare Birthplace Trust.

7

ON SACKS &
SHERRIS

Porter. ...it provokes the desire, but it takes away the performance.
Macbeth, II, iii, 29

HAKESPEARE HAD relatively few kind words to say about the effects of alcohol; most often he portrayed its actions as side-effects, and commonly as drunken behaviour in taverns and drinking-houses. This would appear quite reasonable, as the Elizabethan audience enjoyed the sight of drunkenness and revelry on the stage, and the spectacle of a drunk had common appeal. Falstaff, one of Shakespeare's most popular characters, had a lot to say about alcohol. He was typical of a particular kind of soldier, one who spent the money earned from his campaigns in taverns and brothels while looking for new opportunities in forthcoming campaigns. The philosophy of Falstaff was simple: 'The better part of valour is discretion' (1 *King Henry IV,* V, iv, 120) and 'Honour is a mere scutcheon* (V, i, 139). He was a remarkable man; quite out of place at a serious occasion, but a good companion at a rowdy evening. No wonder, therefore, that Falstaff had his own philosophy

---

*A scutcheon was a coat of arms, painted on boards or cloth, which was carried at the funeral of a gentleman and afterwards hung in the church.

on the virtues of alcohol (2 *King Henry IV*, IV, iii, 85):

> I would you had but the wit; 'twere better than your dukedom.
> Good faith, this same young sober-blooded boy doth not love
> me; nor a man cannot make him laugh – but that's no marvel;
> he drinks no wine. There's never none of these demure boys
> come to any proof;[1] for thin drink doth so over-cool their
> blood, and making many fish-meals, that they fall into a kind
> of male green-sickness;[2] and then, when they marry, they get[3]
> wenches. They are generally fools and cowards – which some
> of us should be too, but for inflammation.[4] A good sherris-
> sack[5] hath a twofold operation in it. It ascends me into the
> brain; dries me there all the foolish and dull and crudy[6]
> vapours which environ it; makes it apprehensive, quick,
> forgetive,[7] full of nimble, fiery, and delectable shapes; which
> delivered o'er to the voice, the tongue, which is the birth, be-
> comes excellent wit. The second property of your excellent
> sherris is the warming of the blood; which before, cold and
> settled, left the liver[8] white and pale, which is the badge of
> pusillanimity and cowardice; but the sherris warms it, and
> makes it course from the inwards to the parts extremes. It illu-
> mineth the face, which, as a beacon,* gives warning to all the
> rest of this little kingdom, man, to arm; and then the vital
> commoners and inland petty spirits muster me all to their cap-
> tain, the heart, who, great and puff'd up with this retinue, doth
> any deed of courage – and this valour comes of sherris. So
> that skill in the weapon is nothing without sack, for that sets it
> a-work; and learning, a mere hoard of gold kept by a devil till
> sack commences[9] it and sets it in act and use. Hereof comes it
> that Prince Harry is valiant; for the cold blood he did natural-

---

*Beacon: during the English wars with Spain, beacons were kept ready on all high
points, so that warning of an invasion could be immediately given. The beacons
were lit several times, notably in 1588 to give warning of the approach of the
Spanish Armada.

ly inherit of his father, he hath, like lean, sterile, and bare land, manured, husbanded,[10] and till'd, with excellent endeavour of drinking good and good store of fertile sherris, that he is become very hot and valiant. If I had a thousand sons, the first humane principle I would teach them should be to forswear thin potations, and to addict themselves to sack.

This may be Falstaff's philosophy, but elsewhere an entirely different view is expressed. Octavius Caesar declines to respond to a toast to him that is proposed by Antony (*Antony and Cleopatra*, II, vii, 95):

Antony. Here's to Caesar!
Caesar.   I could well forbear't.
It's monstrous[11] labour when I wash my brain[12]
And it grows fouler.

Under the influence of alcohol, Cassio, Othello's lieutenant, gets himself into trouble, and when he sobers up is ashamed of himself, realising that it may have affected his reputation (*Othello*, II, iii, 279):

Oh God, that men should put an enemy in their mouths to steal away their brains! That we should with joy, pleasance,[13] revel, and applause, transform ourselves into beasts!

Lady Macbeth plans to get King Duncan's attendants drunk as part of her ambitious design (*Macbeth*, I, vii, 65):

That memory, the warder[14] of the brain,
Shall be a fume, and the receipt of reason
A limbec[15] only.*

---

*Memory, which keeps watch in the brain, will be confused by the fumes of drink, and reason becomes like a still (limbec), distilling only confused thoughts.

A humble porter tells the great Macduff that drink 'is a great provoker of three things' (II, iii, 28):

> Lechery, sir, it provokes and it unprovokes; it provokes the desire, but it takes away the performance. Therefore much drink may be said to be an equivocator with lechery: it makes him, and it mars him; it sets him on, and it takes him off; it persuades him, and disheartens him; makes him stand to, and not stand to; in conclusion, equivocates him in a sleep, and, giving him the lie, leaves him.

Harsh words are said about drunken behaviour:
By Hamlet (I, iv, 19):

> They clepe[16] us drunkards, and with swinish[17] phrase
> Soil our addition;[18] and, indeed, it takes
> From our achievements, though perform'd at height,
> The pith and marrow of our attribute.

By Cassio when he is sober (*Othello, II, iii, 280*):

> Drunk! And speak parrot! And quabble, swagger, swear! And discourse fustian[19] with one's own shadow! O though invisible spirit of wine, if thou hast no name to be known by, let us call thee devil!

By a philosopher at one of Timon's banquets (*Timon of Athens,* I, ii, 130):

> We make ourselves fools to disport ourselves,
> And spend our flatteries to drink those men
> Upon whose age we void it up again
> With poisonous spite and envy.

By a clown (*Twelfth Night,* I, v, 122):

> *Olivia.* What's a drunken man like, fool?

Gadshill (Edward Atienza), Francis (Timothy Harley), Falstaff
(Anthony Quayle), and Bardolph (Michael Bates), in Act II, Scene IV,
of a production of *King Henry IV, Part I*, by the Shakespeare Memorial
Theatre in 1951. Photograph by Angus McBean; reproduced by
courtesy of The Shakespeare Birthplace Trust.

Clown. Like a drown'd man, a fool, and a madman: one draught
above heat makes him a fool; the second mads him; and a
third drowns him.

By the crazy Timon (IV, iii, 427):

Go, suck the subtle blood o' th' grape
Till the high fever seethe your blood to froth.

[119]

In a few brief words Shakespeare summarised a situation which unfortunately is seen far too commonly (*Love's Labour's Lost*, IV, iii, 46):

> *Berowne.* One drunkard loves another of the name.

The familiar swollen, red nose which sometimes develops in heavy beer drinkers was appropriately called the 'burning lamp' by Falstaff, when he accused his companion Bardolph of drinking too much (1 *King Henry IV*, III, iii, 24):

> Do thou amend thy face, and I'll amend my life. Thou art our admiral,* thou bearest the lantern in the poop,[20] but 'tis in the nose of thee; thou art the Knight of the Burning Lamp.

Bardolph had put in many years of imbibing 'sack and sherris', which had probably resulted in the rhinophyma described above. He is not let off easily on this account (*King Henry V*, III, vi, 98):

> *Fluellen.* ... one Bardolph, if your Majesty know the man; his face is all bubukles,[21] and whelks,[22] and knobs, and flames o' fire; and his lips blow at his nose, and it is like a coal of fire, sometimes blue and sometimes red; but his nose is executed and his fire's out.

Caliban, a deformed savage, is allowed to state his case. He advocates a harsh form of therapy for the treatment of alcoholism – substituting brine for alcohol (*The Tempest*, III, ii, 61):

> ... give him blows,

---

*The admiral's ship, which led the fleet, carried a lighted lantern by night so that the fleet could keep together.

And take his bottle from him. When that's gone
He shall drink naught but brine …

Much of the stuff is consumed on social occasions, as a means of passing time, or for dispelling the 'blues' which are attendant on society's problems (*Merchant of Venice*, I, i, 80):

> *Gratiano*. With mirth and laughter let old wrinkles come;
> And let my liver rather heat with wine
> Than my heart cool with mortifying groans.

Recognising this situation, Cassio, Othello's honourable lieutenant, expresses his weakness (*Othello*, II, iii, 29):

> I have very poor and unhappy brains for drinking; I could well wish courtesy[23] would invent some other custom of entertainment.

However, Iago urges that alcohol has advantages if taken in moderation – with which most people would agree (*Othello*, II, iii, 300):

> Come, come, good wine is a good familiar creature, if it be well us'd; exclaim no more against it.

Juliet (Estelle Kohler) and Friar Laurence (Tony Church)
in a production of *Romeo and Juliet* by the Royal
Shakespeare Theatre in 1973. From The Shakespeare
Birthplace Trust, Shakespeare Centre Library.

8
DRUGS, HERBS
& POISONS

Friar Lawrence. O, mickle is the powerful grace that lies
In plants, herbs, stones and their true qualities;
For nought so vile that on the earth doth live
But to the earth some special good doth give ...
Romeo and Juliet, II, iii,15

RIAR LAWRENCE, who spoke the foregoing lines in *Romeo and Juliet,* was an example of the traditional priest-physician-apothecary, who was considered to have knowledge of the use of herbs and drugs, as well as the means of curing those who sought his help. In those days, many drugs which were in common use were known to an educated layman, but some were so dangerous and toxic as to be used only by the very brave or the desperately ill. These drugs, and their effects, provided considerable entertainment on the stage, especially to whip up excitement in scenes of suicide or poisoning. Most of the 'drugs' mentioned in Shakespeare's plays would be quite unfamiliar to the average person today. Grocers and apothecaries at one stage in history were united into one company as a body of general traders. Apothecaries purchased their drugs from a wandering army of 'green men and women', who scoured the countryside looking for medicinal roots and herbs. By the sixteenth century, with the help of an edict promulgated by

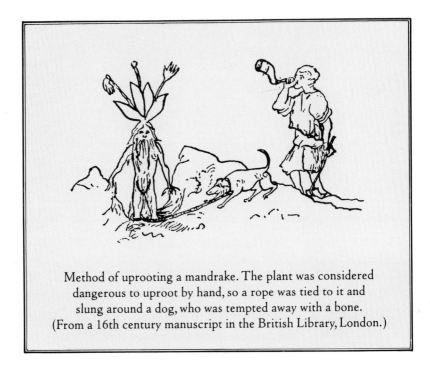

Method of uprooting a mandrake. The plant was considered dangerous to uproot by hand, so a rope was tied to it and slung around a dog, who was tempted away with a bone. (From a 16th century manuscript in the British Library, London.)

King James I, apothecaries had dissociated themselves from the grocers and formed their own guild. Hence we came to hear about the deadly nightshade or belladonna, monkshood or aconitum, foxglove or digitalis, hemlock or conium, mandrake or mandragora, henbane or hyoscyamus, and many others.

Shakespeare is cautious in his description of drugs and herbs – and so he should be, as he mentions quite a number.*

---

*According to Rydén, the total number of plant references in Shakespeare's works approximates 775, and they run the whole gamut from fungi, mosses (in a popular sense) and ferns to flowering plants (Rydén, M., Shakespearean Plant Names, *Acta Univ. Stockh.*, 1978.)

The Duke of Burgundy, in *King Henry V,* (V, ii, 39) makes a remarkable comparison between the disordered state of France and a disused garden:

And all her husbandry[1] doth lie on heaps,
Corrupting in its own fertility.
Her vine, the merry cheerer of the heart,
Unpruned dies;   her hedges even-pleach'd,
Like prisoners wildly overgrown with hair,
Put forth disorder'd twigs; her fallow leas[2]
The darnel, hemlock, and rank fumitory
Doth root upon, while that the coulter[3] rusts
That should deracinate[4] such savagery;
The even mead,[5] that erst brought sweetly forth
The freckled cowslip, burnet,[6] and green clover,
Wanting the scythe, all uncorrected, rank,
Conceives by idleness, and nothing teems
But hateful docks, rough thistles, kecksies,[7] burs,
Losing both beauty and utility.

All the herbs and weeds mentioned in this garden of France are not medicinal, but nevertheless the Duke mentions several that are – darnel, hemlock, fumitory, cowslip, burnet, cloves, docks, thistles, kecksies, burs.

The hemlock, derived from *Conium maculatum,* was historically the main ingredient of the Athenian State poison. The ancient Greeks used a brew made from hemlock as a method of execution for criminals condemned to death. The philosopher Socrates (400 B.C.) was sentenced to death on the grounds that he disregarded religious traditions, and was executed by being made to drink a cup of poisonous hemlock. Hemlock was introduced into medicine by Dioscor-

The vertues of Dog=
gis tonge.

He roote layd to wyth oyle, heleth woundes: wyth barly mele it heleth faynt Antonies fyer, the fame yf a man be anoynted wyth it and wyth oyle, prouoketh fweate. Fuchsius grueth thefe properties vnto the common doggis tonge: whyche I recken to be lycopfis. It heleth the allmofte incurable fores of the mouth and of other places. It is good for the bloudy flyr, therefore it oughte to be vfed agaynft all fores and woundes, and agaynft the frenche por, and fuch lyke difeafes. It helpeth also the iffue of feed, and catarrhes: where= fore thys herbe is put in to the pilles, whyche are good for euery catar, or rewm. Now feyng that the properties that Diofcorides grueth vn= to lycopfis, are lyke vnto them that the common doggis tonge hath: and the lyknes do very well agree: wee may the more boldly pronunce, that lycopfis is our common doggis tonge.

[marginal handwritten notes: Antonius fyer smal. flie, fueurso por catarrh/oo rewme:]

Of Eglentine or fwete brere.
Rubus canis.

Glentine is named in Greke kynorho= dos: in Latine rofa canina : in Duche wyld rofen: in fren= che rofe fauuage: or eglentier. The egle= tine is much like the common brere but the leues are fwete and plea= faunt to fmel to, as the brere or hep tree leues are not. There is com= monly a fpongious ball founde in the eglentine bufhe as Plini wry= teth.

The vertues
of Eglentine.

Lini wryteth in the.xxv booke of hys naturall hi= ftory, that the roote of eglentine is good againft the bytynge of a mad dog: and that the fpongious ball that groweth in the bufhe burned in to pouder, is good to fyll vp that is fallen from the head by the red fcal. Eglentine femeth to haue been fyrft called in Greke kynorhodos becaufe: the roote heled them that were bytten of a mad dog.

[marginal handwritten note: a madd dogo]

Cynos

Dog's tongue and eglantine (sweet – briar), from *A newe herball* by W. A. Turner, London, 1551. (From *A Catalogue of Sixteenth Century Medical Books in Edinburgh Libraries,* compiled by D. T. Bird, 1982; reproduced by courtesy of the Royal College of Physicians of Edinburgh.)

ides* for the external treatment of erysipelas and herpes. Pliny and Avicenna† also considered it a useful drug for the treatment of tumours, and later it was used in various neurological conditions such as epilepsy, mania and chorea.

Henbane *(Hyoscyamus niger)* is another plant with a long medicinal history. It is deadly when eaten by poultry – hence its popular name. The name 'hyoscyamus', however, comes from the Greek, meaning 'hog bean'. At various times it was considered a love potion, a magical herb and an ingredient of witches' brew. It was used in a wide range of nervous and painful conditions which required sedation and analgesia and is probably one of the oldest narcotics in the world. In surgical practice, hyoscine (hyoscyamus) is given by injection for anaesthesia, and in combination with morphine is used to induce 'twilight sleep'. In *Hamlet*, we are told by the ghost of Hamlet's father that he was poisoned by the 'juice of cursed hebona', poured into his ear! Hebona is probably henbane; the ghost tells Hamlet (I, v, 61):

Upon my secure hour[8] thy uncle stole,
With juice of cursed hebona in a vial,
And in the porches[9] of my ears did pour
The leperous distilment ...

---

*Pedanios Dioscorides (first century after Christ) an eminent physician of antiquity, served in the army under Nero. He was famous for his book *De materia medica*, an early pharmacopoeia or listing of drugs. His work on this subject remained for centuries the standard authority.

†Pliny (A.D. 23-79) was the first to suggest the association between thyroid disease and water when he reported that water from some wells produced goitre. He was the author of *Natural History*, an immense encyclopaedic work. Avicenna (980-1037), a Persian physician, composed a great encyclopaedia of medical knowledge, the *Canon*, which served as the main textbook of medicine, both among the Arabic-speaking people and in the west, till the seventeenth century.

The ghost goes on to tell how swiftly the poisonous substance acted:

> ... whose effect
> Holds such an enmity with blood of man
> That swift as quicksilver it courses through
> The natural gates and alleys of the body;
> And with a sudden vigour it doth posset[10]
> And curd, like eager[11] droppings into milk,
> The thin and wholesome blood.

Aconite or monkshood, a poisonous extract from the
plant *Aconitum napellus,* or wolf's-bane, is also referred to in
its lethal sense. A poisonous herb, it was used as an arrow
poison by ancient Chinese. Later, it was used in mediaeval
medicine for feverish conditions, and more recently it was
used to make an anodyne liniment for the treatment of
sciatica and neuralgia. King Henry IV tells of its venom (2
King Henry IV, IV, iv, 47):

> ... though it do work as strong
> As aconitum or rash gunpowder.

The herb fumiter *(Fumaria officinalis)* was credited with
having rare and weird properties. Legend says that it arose
from emanations from the ground, and not from seeds.
When burned, its smoke repelled evil spirits. Its common
and botanical names are derived from the Latin word for
smoke. From earlier times, fumiter was considered useful in
conditions of intestinal obstruction and skin diseases. It was
formerly boiled in milk 'for blotches, weals and pustules',
besides being useful for 'melancholy'. Apart from its being
one of the weeds in the overgrown 'French garden' (*King*

The apothecary (Jost Amman). The apothecaries
formed their own company, and apart from
dispensing medicine, they also practised as general
practitioners. Reproduced from *Medicine and the
Artist (Ars Medica)* by permission of the
Philadelphia Museum of Art; Dover Publications,
Inc., New York.

Ellen Terry as Ophelia in *Hamlet* (Act IV, Scene V).
From *The Complete Works of William Shakespeare* (c. 1910).
Photograph by Window & Grove, London.

Henry V, V, ii, 45), Shakespeare included 'rank fumiter' with other wild herbs and weeds – hardock, hemlock, nettles, cuckoo-flowers, darnel – in the crown of weeds worn by the demented King Lear (IV, iv, 2):

> As mad as the vex'd sea, ...
> Crown'd with rank fumiter and furrow weeds,
> With hardocks, hemlock, nettles, cuckoo-flow'rs
> Darnel, and all the idle weeds that grow
> In our sustaining[12] corn.

The colocynth or bitter apple, *Citrullus colocynthis,* provided a purgative drug which was prepared from the dried fruit of a plant from the gourd family commonly called coloquintida. It is spoken of by Iago in *Othello* (I, iii, 356):

> The food that to him now is as luscious as locusts shall be to him shortly as acerbe as the coloquintida.

It is not known which luscious fruit Shakespeare called the 'locusts', whereas we know that the coloquintida is the 'bitter apple'.

In the language of flowers, each had its own peculiar meaning. Ophelia in *Hamlet,* (IV, v, 172) a pathetic character who went mad and later committed suicide, distributed various flowers appropriately; for her brother she provided rosemary (remembrance) and pansies (thoughts); for the King, fennel (flattery) and columbine (thanklessness); for the Queen rue, also called the herb of grace (sorrow), and daisy (light of love). Neither the King nor the Queen is worthy of violets (faithfulness):

> *Ophelia.* There's rosemary, that's for remembrance; pray you, love, remember. And there is pansies, that's for thoughts.

Laertes. A document in madness – thoughts and remembrance
fitted.
Ophelia. There's fennel for you, and columbines.
There's rue for you; and here's some for me.
We may call it herb of grace a Sundays.
O, you must wear your rue with a difference.
There's a daisy. I would give you some violets, but they
wither'd all when my father died.

Rosemary (remembrance) was also used as an emblem at
funerals and weddings. Friar Lawrence in *Romeo and Juliet*
(IV, v, 79) says:

Dry up your tears, and stick your rosemary
On this fair corse,[13]...

And Perdita in *The Winter's Tale* (IV, iv, 74): says:

For you there's rosemary and rue; these keep
Seeming and savour[14] all the winter long.

Moving away from the beautiful language of flowers,
Shakespeare frequently referred to the dreaded mandrake
(Mandragora officiarum). This was a typical example of drug
abuse of a medicinal plant, and was especially used by those
obsessed with magical rites and orgiastic rituals. Mandrake,
together with some other hallucinogenic and narcotic herbs,
was closely associated with the Dark Ages. In its early
history it was protected by Greek collectors, who invested
the root with fictitious and harmful attributes, such as its
ability to kill the person who pulled it from the ground or
even to drive him crazy. No wonder it was a standard
component of witches' brew! It was supposed to be useful as
a sedative, purgative and emetic, to have effects on the
nervous system, and to be an hallucinogenic and aphrodisiac.

Fanciful woodcut of the mandrake root, from *The grete herball*, London, 1526. The screams of this powerful plant were believed to kill anyone who pulled it from the ground. It had some vague resemblance to the human form. (From *A Catalogue of Sixteenth Century Medical Books in Edinburgh Libraries*, compiled by D. T. Bird, 1982; reproduced by courtesy of the Royal College of Physicians of Edinburgh).

An ointment was made from the root for the treatment of ulcers. The root of the mandrake is forked, and the whole plant was vaguely supposed to resemble the human form. As the plant was supposed to utter a cry when pulled from the ground, and those who heard it would go insane or die, it was uprooted by tying the stem to a dog and then tempting him away with a bone. The dreadful shrieks heard when the plant was uprooted are referred to in *Romeo and Juliet* (IV, iii, 47):

Juliet. And shrieks like mandrakes' torn out of the earth,

[133]

That living mortals, hearing them, run mad.

With regard to the decoction which was used as a narcotic, Cleopatra, separated from her lover, says in desperation (*Antony and Cleopatra*, I, v, 4):

Cleopatra. ... Give me to drink mandragora.
Charmian.   Why, Madam?
Cleopatra. That I may sleep out this great gap of time
My Antony is away.

As an hypnotic, Iago mentions it as follows (*Othello*, III, iii, 334):

                    Not poppy nor mandragora,
Nor all the drowsy syrups of the world,
Shall ever medicine thee to that sweet sleep
Which thou owed'st yesterday.

Mandragora was supposed to have enhanced action if the decoction was made from a plant growing over the buried remains of human beings, and especially those of executed criminals! It was certainly a plant to be feared and used with great caution. Falstaff refers to its human shape when he abuses his servant (2 *King Henry IV*, I, ii, 16):

Thou whoreson mandrake, thou art fitter to be worn in my cap than to wait at my heels.

And again, when he contemptuously describes Justice Shallow (III, ii, 324):

'A was the very genius of famine; yet lecherous as a monkey, and the whores call'd him mandrake.

[134]

The groan or cry when the plant was pulled out from the ground was, of course, the most fearsome of its properties, and a further allusion to this belief is made in the lines spoken by Suffolk (2 *King Henry VI*, III, ii, 309):

> Wherefore should I curse them?
> Would curses kill as doth the mandrake's groan,
> I would invent as bitter searching terms,
> As curst, as harsh, and horrible to hear.

The extent of superstition in Shakespeare's day can be estimated from the several references to the mandrake which exceed the number of allusions to any other 'drug'. Hallucinatory herbs and their products have been used for thousands of years in all civilizations. Their abuse in our own times is a topic of much contention in what is known as the 'drug problem'. Opium, hashish, cannabis, morphine and cocaine are all derived from plants or herbs.

Shakespeare adapted a great deal from Holinshed's Chronicles in the construction of many plays, and *Macbeth* was among them. When he used the expression 'the insane root' in *Macbeth* (I, iii, 84) – 'Or have we eaten of the insane root that takes the reason prisoner?' – it has been thought that he had the root of some particular plant in mind. Hemlock, mandrake, belladonna, or henbane has each in turn been considered to be the root referred to. No one can be sure. However, it must be acknowledged in favour of belladonna that the symptoms of intoxication produced by the root were graphically described in Holinshed's Chronicles. The deadly nightshade has been known from time immemorial as a most dangerous plant, and it was exceedingly com-

The physician visiting the apothecary: from
Brunschwig's *Chirurgia*, 1497. (From *A History of
Medicine* by A. Castiglioni, 1941.)

mon in Europe a few centuries ago. Shakespeare adapted everything that came his way to the dramatic necessities of the play.

Sickness in primitive societies was often attributed to supernatural forces entering the body, and therefore medicine was often linked with the supernatural. Early doctors and herbalists were invested with a social status of their own, and

Choleric

Above and overleaf: The four humours. The humoral theory had
existed from early Greek civilization. The four fundamental humours
were responsible for health and illness, and Galen's contribution to
this ancient doctrine was to link them to the four basic
temperaments – sanguine, phlegmatic, choleric and melancholic.
(From MS C 54, courtesy of the Zentralbibliothek, Zurich.)

Sanguine

Melancholic

Phlegmatic

often enhanced their position by guarding the secrets of
their herbal remedies. Today, plants still play a vital role in
the tobacco and brewing industries, and others, like ginseng,
of unproven therapeutic value, are in great demand.

Some medicines were also derived from metals and
minerals. Cerimon, the physician in *Pericles,* mentions this
(III, ii, 33):

> I have,
> Together with my practice, made familiar
> To me and to my aid the blest infusions
> That dwell in vegetives, in metals, stones;
> And I can speak of the disturbances
> That nature works, and of her cures ...

Cymbeline was a play which concerned the misfortunes of
a faithful lady who was scorned, maligned and ill-treated by
her lover. In true mediaeval fashion she escaped a most difficult situation by taking a powerful drug (IV, ii, 327):

> *Belarius.* The drug he gave me, which he said was precious
> And cordial to me, have I not found it
> Murd'rous to the senses?

Death by poisoning was popular on the stage. Romeo
knew exactly what he wanted when he asked a poor apothecary for a powerful poison (*Romeo and Juliet,* V, i, 59):

> let me have
> A dram of poison, such soon-speeding gear[15]
> As will disperse itself through all the veins
> That the life-weary taker may fall dead,
> And that the trunk[16] may be discharg'd of breath
> As violently as hasty powder fir'd
> Doth hurry from the fatal cannon's womb.

In the same play, Friar Lawrence predicted that the poison which he had given Juliet would produce a complete cessation of all vital functions, and, like a time-clock, would allow her to return to life at an appointed hour (IV, i, 93):

Friar Lawrence. Take thou this vial, being then in bed,
And this distilled liquor drink thou off;
When presently through all thy veins shall run
A cold and drowsy humour; for no pulse
Shall keep his native progress, but surcease;
No warmth, no breath, shall testify thou livest;
The roses in they lips and cheeks shall fade
To paly ashes, thy eyes' windows fall,
Like death when he shuts up the day of life;
Each part, depriv'd of supple government,
Shall, stiff and stark and cold, appear like death;
And in this borrow'd likeness of shrunk death
Thou shalt continue two and forty hours,
And then awake as from a pleasant sleep.

The drug worked as the Friar predicted, which is evident from Capulet's words when he sees Juliet (IV, v, 25):

Capulet. Ha! let me see her. Out, alas! she's cold;
Her blood is settled, and her joints are stiff.
Life and these lips have long been parted.

Shakespeare's clinical descriptions of the action of poisons are realistic; the death of King John is a notable example of this (V, vii, 34):

Prince Henry. How fares your Majesty?
King John. Poison'd – ill-fare! Dead, forsook, cast off;
And none of you will bid the winter come
To thrust his icy fingers in my maw.[17]
Nor let my kingdom's rivers take their course

Galenicals: 16th century woodcut showing the preparation
of theriac, a universal panacea. (From H. Brunschwig, *Das neu distiller Buch*,
Strassburg, 1537; in the National Library of Medicine, Bethesda.)

Through my burn'd bosom, nor entreat the north
To make his bleak winds kiss my parched lips
And comfort me with cold.

And finally, with few words, an important therapeutic
connection is summarised (2 *King Henry IV*, I, i 137):

> *Northumberland.* In poison there is physic ...

[139]

Plato and Aristotle. The philosopher Plato (c.
420-347 B.C.), a student of Socrates, was probably
a contemporary of Hippocrates and was a teacher
of Aristotle. Aristotle (384-322 B.C.) had a
lasting influence on medicine, as his methods were
based on careful observations of both humans and animals.

9
THE ELEMENTS
& THE
HUMOURS

Sir Toby Belch. Does not our lives consist of the four elements?*
Twelfth Night, II, iii, 9

T WAS IN VERY ANCIENT TIMES, and possibly in connection with observations of secretions and excretions from the human body (which impressed the imagination of primitive man), that the concept of humoral pathology was born. This was elevated to the level of a scientific theory by Hippocrates (460-377 B.C.), the greatest of our ancient masters. Humoral pathology, however, was definitely established in the works of Galen (A.D. 129-200), and survived the storms and stresses of centuries to last up to the Renaissance period. It was the accepted belief in Shakespeare's time, as it was in the preceding centuries, that all matter in the universe consisted of four basic elements – earth, air, fire and water. They were considered hostile to each other, but could exist in harmony when in proper proportions. The human body was also matter, and

---

*The next two lines after this quotation appear in rather different context and read: 'Faith, so they say; but I think it rather consists of eating and drinking'.

hence considered to be composed of the same four elements. When anatomists or other learned men studied the human body, they observed its quality of dampness or all-pervading *humour*. But the humours of the body were obviously of different kinds, and on the assumption that the physical body must be composed of four elements, 'earth' was identified as 'black bile', 'air' as 'blood', 'fire' as 'choler', and 'water' as 'phlegm'. Each element produced a corresponding temperament, which was expressed as a man's 'complexion'. An excess of earth produced the *melancholic* humour, which was cold and dry; an excess of air the *sanguine* humour, which was hot and moist; an excess of fire the *choleric* humour, which was hot and dry; and an excess of water the *phlegmatic* humour, which was cold and moist. In a healthy body the four humours were perfectly balanced and in harmony with each other. However, if one or more humours was predominant or deficient, the individual became physically ill or mentally unbalanced. The humoral pathology explained all known diseases as caused by a mixture of the four cardinal humours.

Shakespeare mentioned all the humours in his plays, using them in different contexts and with a wide range of meanings. He knew which humour was akin to which of the four elements and, not infrequently, used the humours and elements interchangeably, as though he believed they were the same. More frequently, he associated organs with emotions: spite with the spleen; compassion with the bowels; love with the heart; and lust and courage with the liver. In one instance in his plays he mentioned melancholy as a 'surly spirit', and once he used the phrase 'spirit of humours', thus showing a possible confusion between the four

[142]

humours of the Pythagorean school and the three spirits of the Galenic physiology. By 'spirit' the vital spirit or *pneuma* is usually implied; the term is correctly used in *Love's Labour's Lost* in the phrase 'the nimble spirits in the arteries', an idea which is again repeated in *Twelfth Night* in the words 'Let thy blood and spirit embrace'. Though 'humour' was commonly used to imply one of the four humours, its most common meanings were mood, obsession, whim or temperament.

On the 'melancholic' humour, a despondent King John tells his lords (III, iii, 41):

> Or if that surly spirit, melancholy,
> Had bak'd thy blood and made it heavy-thick,
> Which else runs tickling up and down the veins,
> Making that idiot, laughter, keep men's eyes
> And strain their cheeks to idle merriment,
> A passion hateful to my purposes...

Of the 'sanguine' humour we read in the following quotations:

> *Basset.* This fellow here, with envious carping tongue,
> Upbraided me about the rose[1] I wear,
> Saying the sanguine colour of the leaves
> Did represent my master's blushing cheeks...
> *King Henry VI,* IV, i, 90

> *Aaron.* What, what, ye sanguine,[2] shallow-hearted boys!
> Ye white-lim'd walls!
> *Titus Andronicus,* IV, ii, 97

> *Cymbeline.* Upon his neck a mole, a sanguine star;[3]
> It was a mark of wonder.
> *Cymbeline,* V, v, 364

[143]

The forty-seventh aphorism of Hippocrates, section 6, states that 'persons who are benefited by venesection or purging should be bled or purged in spring.' On 'choler', King Richard indulges in an elaborate metaphor, also reminding his lords that certain days and seasons, taken from the almanac, were considered more favourable than others for blood-letting (*King Richard II*, I, i, 153):

> Let's purge this choler[4] without letting blood –
> This we prescribe, though no physician;
> Deep malice makes too deep incision.
> Forget, forgive; conclude[5] and be agreed:
> Our doctors say this is no month to bleed.

And Hamlet tells his courtiers (III, ii, 298):

> ...signify this to his doctor; for me to put him
> to his purgation[6] would perhaps plunge him
> into far more choler.

It was quite acceptable for a person to talk of his humour. Indeed, it was the mark of a would-be intellectual to have a humour, preferably a melancholic humour, which strangely was the sign of a cultured mind. The 'melancholic' individual had certain characteristics. Typically, he was a man out of touch with his surroundings, who made himself known by wearing a large black hat with the brim pulled down over his brow, and a cloak, and by possessing a general air of moody aloofness.

There were three types of melancholic humour: lover's melancholy, malcontent's (or politician's) melancholy, and intellectual melancholy. The melancholic lover was described by Rosalind when she criticised Orlando for not having the

Orlando (Michael Williams), Rosalind (Dorothy Tutin), and Celia
(Janet Suzman), in Act III, Scene II, of a production of *As You Like It* by
the Royal Shakespeare Theatre in 1967. Photograph from The
Shakespeare Birthplace Trust, Shakespeare Centre Library.

genuine marks of the melancholic (*As You Like It*, III, ii,
345):

> *Orlando.* What were his marks?
> *Rosalind.* A lean cheek, which you have not;
> a blue eye and sunken,[7] which you have not;
> an unquestionable[8] spirit, which you have not;
> a beard neglected, which you have not;
> but I pardon you for that, for simply your having
> in beard is a younger brother's revenue.[9]
> Then your hose should be ungarter'd, your
> bonnet unbanded,[10] your sleeve unbutton'd,
> your shoe untied, and everything about you
> demonstrating a careless desolation.

[145]

'The Chemist', by David Teniers the Younger. As depicted in this
engraving, the chemist was often also an alchemist and a
medical practitioner. (Courtesy of Bibliothèque Nationale, Paris.)

The malcontent (or political melancholic) was also fairly
common. Thersites (*Troilus and Cressida*) was a good example; he was described as a frustrated individual who took his
revenge on the world by criticising and imputing the worst
motives to every action (II, iii, 23):

> The common curse of mankind, folly and ignorance,
> be thine in great revenue! Heaven bless thee from
> a tutor, and discipline come not near thee!

The third type was the intellectual melancholic, and his
was the true type of melancholic humour. Hamlet is a classic
example of this humour, and his famous soliloquoy 'To be or
not to be' (III, i, 56) sums up the problems of the intellectual
melancholic. He was a man who believed that the times were
evil, and who could see no remedy or hope in either this

world or the next – if, indeed, there was a next (III, i, 76):

> Who would these fardels bear,
> To grunt and sweat under a weary life,
> But that the dread of something after death –
> The undiscover'd country from whose bourn[11]
> No traveller returns – puzzles the will,[12]
> And makes us rather bear those ills we have
> Than fly to others that we know not of?

Melancholy was well recognised as a disease, and many treatises had been written by physicians of those days discussing its symptoms, causes and cures – which probably led to this humour being the 'in thing'.

One of the many causes of melancholy was the presence of bad smells in the environment, a not uncommon situation in the London of those days. This led a contemporary writer, John Harrington, to connect melancholy with the Greek hero Ajax.* Ajax, in Shakespeare's *Troilus and Cressida,* was a Grecian commander, but a foolish one and a great boaster. In 1596 John Harrington wrote a book called *The Metamorphosis of Ajax,* which was in fact a treatise on domestic sanitation. He used the name 'Ajax' for the privy, and to describe his invention of the first water closet. 'Jakes' was synonymous with a privy, and 'Ajax' was probably a pun upon 'a jakes'. In *King Lear (II, ii, 60),* Kent, in reference to Oswald, says, 'I will tread this unbolted villain into mortar, and daub the wall of a jakes with him'. Harrington's book caused some amusement, and for some time the name 'Ajax' usually connoted both a privy and the melancholic humour.

---

*Ajax was a legendary hero who fought on the Greek side in the Trojan war. He was considered the bravest of Greeks next to Achilles.

Sarah Bernhardt as Hamlet in *Hamlet* (Act I,
Scene V). From *The Complete Works of William
Shakespeare* (c. 1910). Photograph: Otto, Paris.

10
'LIFE'S A MIRACLE'

Miranda.   O brave new world
That has such people in't!
The Tempest, V, i, 183

IFE IS ONE OF THE great mysteries of the universe, and philosophers and scholars have pondered over its meaning since ancient times. It has no simple definition, but nevertheless, Shakespeare expressed his thoughts about it with extreme literary ability. In the fairy-tale story of *The Tempest,* the Lady Miranda, passing from courtship to high romance, tells her lover (V, i, 181):

O, wonder!
How many goodly creatures are there here!
How beauteous mankind is!

Life and death are intimately linked together. In the field of battle, the Duke of York has realised that fortune has turned against him (3 *King Henry VI,* I, iv, 25):

The sands[1] are numb'red that make up my life;
Here must I stay, and here my life must end.

And the rebellious Northumberland, fearing the worst, says (*King Richard II,* II, i, 270):

...even through the hollow eyes of death
I spy life peering;...

The uncertainty of life, and its attendant illnesses and hazards, are described by the crazy Timon in an invocation to a higher being (V, i, 196):

...ease them of their griefs,
Their fears of hostile strokes, their aches, losses,
Their pangs of love, with other incident² throes
That nature's fragile vessel doth sustain
In life's uncertain voyage.

One of Shakespeare's most beautiful descriptions of a tranquil life, blessed with peace and serenity, is given by King Henry VI. Standing alone in a battlefield, surrounded by dead comrades and enemies, he reflects on how wonderful it would be for him to have a peaceful life. He describes the carefree life of a humble shepherd, planning his days and hours and taking his time doing so. Nothing could be more secure and enjoyable than this simple life – one which should be recommended to all patients, and even possessed by ourselves! (3 *King Henry VI*, II, iv, 21):

O God! Methinks it were a happy life
To be no better than a homely swain;³
To sit upon a hill, as I do now,
To carve out dials quaintly, point by point,⁴
Thereby to see the minutes how they run –
How many makes the hour full complete,
How many hours brings about the day,
How many days will finish up the year,
How many years a mortal man may live.
When this is known, then to divide the times –
So many hours must I tend my flock;
So many hours must I take my rest;
So many hours must I contemplate;

So many hours must I sport myself;
So many days my ewes have been with young;
So many weeks ere the poor fools will ean;[5]
So many years ere I shall shear the fleece;
So minutes, hours, days, months and years,
Pass'd over to the end they were created,
Would bring white hairs unto a quiet grave.
Ah, what a life were this! how sweet! how lovely!
Gives not the hawthorn bush a sweeter shade
To shepherds looking on their silly sheep,
Than doth a rich embroider'd canopy
To kings that fear their subjects' treachery?
O yes, it doth; a thousand-fold it doth.
And to conclude: the shepherd's homely curds,[6]
His cold thin drink out of his leather bottle,
His wonted sleep under a fresh tree's shade,
All which secure[7] and sweetly he enjoys,
Is far beyond a prince's delicates[8]–
His viands sparkling in a golden cup,
His body couched in a curious[9] bed,
Where care, mistrust, and treason waits on him.

Jaques' famous speech on the seven ages of man (*As You Like It*, II, vii, 139), beginning 'All the world's a stage', was probably inspired by the motto of the new Globe Theatre (which was first opened to acting in 1599), *Totus mundus agit histrionem* – 'The whole world plays an actor'. In this there are glimpses of the art of medicine:

All the world's a stage,
And all the men and women merely players;
They have their exits and their entrances;
And one man in his time plays many parts,
His acts being seven ages. At first the infant,
Mewling[10] and puking in the nurse's arms;

[151]

Jaques (Max Adrian) in a production of *As You Like it* by the
Shakespeare Memorial Theatre in 1961. Photograph by Angus
McBean; reproduced by courtesy of The Shakespeare Birthplace Trust.

Then the whining school-boy, with his satchel
And shining morning face, creeping like snail
Unwillingly to school. And then the lover,
Sighing like furnace, with a woeful ballad[11]
Made to his mistress' eyebrow. Then a soldier,
Full of strange oaths, and bearded like the pard,[12]
Jealous in honour,[13] sudden and quick in quarrel,
Seeking the bubble reputation[14]
Even in the cannon's mouth. And then the justice,
In fair round belly with good capon lin'd,[15]
With eyes severe and beard of formal cut,[16]
Full of wise saws[17] and modern instances;[18]
And so he plays his part. The sixth age shifts
Into the lean and slipper'd pantaloon,[19]
With spectacles on nose and pouch on side,
His youthful hose, well sav'd, a world too wide
For his shrunk shank; and his big manly voice,
Turning again toward childish treble, pipes
And whistles in his sound. Last scene of all,
That ends this strange eventful history,
Is second childishness and mere oblivion;
Sans teeth, sans eyes, sans taste, sans everything.

In *King Lear*, Edgar attempts to prevent Gloucester from committing suicide by jumping off a cliff, telling him 'Thy life's a miracle' (IV, vi, 55).

Sir Henry Irving as the King in *King Lear* (Act I,
Scene I). From *The Complete Works of William
Shakespeare* (c. 1910). Photograph from the
drawing by J. Bernard Partridge.

11
GERIATRICS

Edgar. The oldest hath borne most; we that are young
Shall never see so much nor live so long.
King Lear, V, iii, 325

ANY ASPECTS OF OLD AGE are considered in Shakespeare's plays. He deals with the traditional wisdom of old age, the deterioration that sets in with advancing years, and old age in good as well as in poor health. He talks about old people hanging on 'for grim death', as well as giving way to youth and the next generation.

Polixenes, the King of Bohemia, disguised himself and endeavoured to find out his son's opinion of an old man (*The Winter's Tale* IV, iv, 386). His son, Prince Florizel, was a young man of considerable personality who would brave his father and, in traditional manner, would even sacrifice a kingdom for his principles:

> *Polixenes.* Methinks a father
> Is at the nuptial of his son a guest
> That best becomes the table. Pray you, once more,
> Is not your father grown incapable
> Of reasonable affairs? Is he not stupid
> With age and alt'ring rheums?[1] Can he speak, hear,
> Know man from man, dispute his own estate?
> Lies he not bed-rid, and again does nothing
> But what he did being childish?

[155]

Old Shepherd (James Bree), Perdita (Susan Maryott), Camillo (Paul
Hardwick), Florizel (Dinsdale Landen), and Polixenes (Patrick Allen),
in a production of *The Winter's Tale* by the Shakespeare Memorial
Theatre in 1960. Photograph by Angus McBean; reproduced by
courtesy of The Shakespeare Birthplace Trust.

To this young Florizel replies, describing the ideal situation
when an old person should be fit and in full possession of his
faculties (IV, iv, 394):

   Florizel.   No, good sir;

He has his health and ampler strength indeed
Than most have of his age.

To Shakespeare, the psychological aspects of old age were
generally its more pleasing side, and he presented these increasingly in his later plays. However, even in the middle of
his career, in the person of Adam in *As You Like It*, he gave a
full and sympathetic picture of old age – a picture that stres-
sed its maturity and sweetness of character and its struggle to
overcome physical infirmities. Adam is the picture of selfless
loyalty, an old man, who boasts that clean living in his younger
days has stood him in good stead (II, iii, 47):

Though I look old, yet I am strong and lusty;
For in my youth I never did apply
Hot and rebellious liquors in my blood,
Nor did not with unbashful forehead[2] woo
The means[3] of weakness and debility;
Therefore my age is as a lusty winter,
Frosty, but kindly.

However, Adam acknowledges that some help may be needed
from a higher authority (II, iii, 43):

He that doth the ravens feed,
Yea, providently caters for the sparrow,
Be comfort to my age!

Later, the poor old fellow nearly dies of hunger and exhaus-
tion in the Forest of Arden.

The daughters of the ageing King Lear have definite opinions about their aged father. Says Goneril (I, iv, 292):

But let his disposition have that scope
As dotage gives it.

[157]

Says Regan (II, iv, 144):

> O, sir, you are old;
> Nature in you stands on the verge
> Of her confine.⁴ You should be rul'd and led
> By some discretion that discerns your state
> Better than yourself.

In *Much Ado About Nothing,* Constable Dogberry patroniz-ingly describes his colleague Verges (III, iv, 32): 'A good old man, sir, he will be talking; as they say "when the age is in the wit is out". ' Where some degree of mental or physical de-terioration accompanies old age, this unfortunate situation is described in several instances. Falstaff had been a page in the Norfolk household some fifty-five years before, and as pages usually commenced at the age of seven, he must have been over sixty-five. However, he admits only to 'some fifty' years, and declares himself in the 'vaward of youth'. His associates repeatedly call him 'old', and finally, he himself is constrained to admit that he 'grows old'. With wine he tries to heat his blood to youthful fervour. The fat old knight is not only an outrageous boaster, but also a debaucher and a coward (*1 King Henry IV,* III, iii, 3):

> *Falstaff.* Do I not dwindle? Why, my skin hangs about me like an old lady's loose gown; I am withered like an old applejohn.*

---

*applejohn: apples ripened on St John's day, midsummer, but eaten two years later when withered.

[158]

Hamlet tells Polonius, an old man (*Hamlet*, II, ii, 196):

> ...old men have gray beards; that their faces are wrinkled;
> their eyes purging thick amber and plum-tree gum; and that
> they have a plentiful lack of wit, together with most weak
> hams...[5]

A clown tells Hamlet (V, i, 71):

> But age, with his stealing steps,
>   Hath clawed me in his clutch.

Macbeth, 'sick at heart', has this comment (V, iii, 22):

> My way of life[6]
> Is fall'n into the sear,[7] the yellow leaf;
> And that which should accompany old age,
> As honour, love, obedience, troops of friends,
> I must not look to have; but in their stead,
> Curses not loud but deep, mouth-honour, breath,
> Which the poor heart would fain deny, and dare not.

In *The Comedy of Errors*, Adriana says (IV, ii, 19):

> He is deformed, crooked, old and sere,[7]
> Ill-fac'd, worse bodied, shapeless everywhere;
> Vicious, ungentle, foolish, blunt, unkind;
> Stigmatical in making,[8] worse in mind.

The second childhood comes up again – an old man is twice
a child in this dialogue (*Hamlet*, II, ii, 378):

> *Hamlet.* That great baby you see there is not yet out of his
> swaddling clouts.
> *Rosencrantz.* Happily he's the second time come to them; for
> they say an old man is twice a child.

Lear is one of the most pathetic figures in all drama. He fits all the descriptions of old age accompanied by intercurrent illness or associated problems. He is repeatedly called 'old', and as early as the second act, he admits as much to Regan. Indeed, he is 'fourscore and upward', has 'white hair', and is 'infirm' and 'weak' with age even before the middle of the play. Age and mental decay have burnt out the last remnants of his kingly humour, leaving him weak in body (I, i, 292):

> 'Tis the infirmity of his age; ... then must we look from his age to receive not alone the imperfections of long-engraffed condition,[9] but therewithal the unruly waywardness that infirm and choleric years bring with them.

The relentless progression of old age, a condition which must ultimately come to all who live long enough, is described by King Henry V, Shakespeare's ideal king (V, ii, 155):

> A good leg will fall; a straight back will stoop; a black beard will turn white; a curl'd pate will grow bald; a fair face will wither; a full eye will wax hollow. But a good heart ... is the sun and the moon; or, rather, the sun and not the moon – for it shines bright and never changes, but keeps his course truly.

A less popular king, the King of France, in *All's Well That Ends Well*, expresses his own views on his age (V, iii, 39):

> Let's take the instant by the forward top;[10]
> For we are old, and on our quick'st decrees
> Th' inaudible and noiseless foot of Time
> Steals ere we can effect them.

Helena (Zoe Caldwell) and the King of France
(Robert Hardy); from Act II, Scene I, of a
production of *All's Well That Ends Well* by the
Shakespeare Memorial Theatre in 1959.
Photograph by Angus McBean, courtesy of The
Shakespeare Birthplace Trust.

In *King Lear,* Gloucester says (III, iii, 25): 'The younger rises, when the old doth fall.' In *Richard II,* York is 'weak with age', and old Gaunt tells the King that, though the royal mandate can hasten age through sorrow, yet nothing the monarch can do will banish wrinkles.

Placing an old person in a 'convalescent home' is also mentioned in Elizabethan language by Talbot (1 *King Henry VI,* III, ii, 88):

We will bestow[11] you in some better place,
Fitter for sickness and for crazy age.[12]

In the following lines, the declining sexual activities that are associated with old age are probably intended by Hamlet (III, iv, 68):

You cannot call it love; for at your age
The heyday[13] in the blood is tame, it's humble,
And waits upon the judgement ...

The last years of life are accompanied by some deterioration in physical and mental capabilities, while precious memories may still be preserved. Ægeon, a merchant of Syracuse, reflects on this sad situation (*Comedy of Errors,* V, i, 310):

Though now this grained[14] face of mine be hid
In sap-consuming winter's drizzled snow,
And all the conduits of my blood froze up,
Yet hath my night of life some memory,
My wasting lamps[15] some fading glimmer left,
My dull deaf ears a little use to hear;
All these old witnesses – I cannot err –

With a brilliant touch, Shakespeare evokes the pathos of

old age in the words of Friar Lawrence (*Romeo and Juliet*, II, iii, 35):

Care keeps his watch in every old man's eye,
And where care lodges sleep will never lie ...

And in the words of Jaques (*As You Like It*, II, vii, 26):

And so, from hour to hour, we ripe and ripe,
And then, from hour to hour, we rot and rot;
And thereby hangs a tale.

Lily Langtry as Cleopatra in *Antony and Cleopatra*
(Act V, Scene II). From *The Complete Works of
William Shakespeare* (c. 1910). Photograph: Van der
Weyde, London.

12
'THE UNDISCOVER'D COUNTRY'

Feeble. A man can die but once; we owe God a death.
2 *King Henry IV*, III, ii, 228

HAKESPEARE'S DESCRIPTIONS of life and death are unique in their variety and frequency. He was particularly good at portraying deaths from a medical point of view, and often did so, death being the usual finale in many dramas and tragedies. The descriptions of the deaths of Falstaff and King John are among his best in terms of medical appeal. The death of King John is described in incomparable poetry as follows (*King John*, V, vii, 1):

Prince Henry. It is too late; the life of all his blood
Is touch'd curruptibly, and his pure brain,
Which some suppose the soul's frail dwelling-house,
Doth by the idle comments that it makes
Foretell the ending of mortality.[1]

. . .

O vanity of sickness! Fierce extremes
In their countenance will not feel themselves.
Death, having prey'd upon the outward parts,
Leaves them invisible,[2] and his siege is now
Against the mind,[3] the which he pricks and wounds
With many legions of strange fantasies,
Which, in their throng and press to that last hold,

Confound themselves.[4] 'Tis strange that death should sing,
I am the cygnet[5] to this pale faint swan
Who chants a doleful hymn to his own death,[6]
And from the organ-pipe of frailty[7] sings
His soul and body to their lasting rest.

. . .

King John. Ay, marry, now my soul hath elbow-room;
It would not out at windows nor at the doors.[8]
There is so hot a summer in my bosom
That all my bowels crumble up to dust.
I am a scribbled form drawn with a pen
Upon a parchment, and against this fire
Do I shrink up.

The anticipation of death is also frequently referred to, and this is what Shakespeare said of various lords and noble-men:

Lord Talbot. But kings and mightiest potentates must die,
For that's the end of human misery.

1 *King Henry VI,* III, ii, 136

And, again:

Lord Talbot. For ere the glass[9] that now begins to run
Finish the process of his sandy hour,
These eyes that see thee now well coloured
Shall see thee withered, bloody, pale and dead.

1 *King Henry VI,* IV, ii, 35

Earl of Warwick. Why, what is pomp, rule, reign, but earth and dust?
And live we how we can, yet die we must.

3 *King Henry VI,* V, ii, 28

King Richard. Cry woe, destruction, ruin and decay –
The worst is death, and death will have his day.
King Richard II, III, ii, 102

And, again:

King Richard. Mount, mount, my soul! thy seat is up on high;
Whilst my gross flesh sinks downward, here to die.
King Richard II, V, v, iii

Hotspur. Doomsday is near; die all, die merrily.
1 *King Henry IV*, IV, i, 134

Cassius. . . . ready to give up the ghost.
Julius Caesar, V, i, 88

Shakespeare's actual descriptions of a dead body are remarkable, and frequent:

Lord. Grim death, how foul and loathsome is thine image!
Taming of the Shrew, Induction, i, 33

When Juliet is found 'dead' by Romeo:

Death, that hath suck'd the honey of thy breath,
Hath had no power yet upon thy beauty.
Thou are not conquer'd; beauty's ensign yet
Is crimson in thy lips and in thy cheeks,
And death's pale flag is not advanced there.
Romeo and Juliet, V, iii, 92

A prostitute describes the death of Falstaff:

I put my hand into the bed and felt them, and they were cold
as any stone; then I felt to his knees, and so upward and upward, and all was as cold as any stone.
King Henry V, II, iii, 24

[167]

H. Beerbohm Tree as the King in *King Richard II*
(Act I, Scene I). From *The Complete Works of
William Shakespeare* (c. 1910). Photograph:
L. Caswall Smith, London.

A brave death was considered a noble and desirable end to life, and nothing was worse than dying the death of a coward. A comet has, from time immemorial, been regarded as a portent of some natural disaster or as the forerunner of the death of a prominent person, and this is expressed in the following famous lines from *Julius Caesar* (II, ii, 30) (Caesar and his wife, Calphurnia, realise that fate is against him):

> *Calphurnia.* When beggars die there are no comets seen:
> The heavens themselves blaze forth the death of princes.
> *Caesar.* Cowards die many times before their deaths:
> The valiant never taste of death but once,
> Of all the wonders that I yet have heard,
> It seems to me most strange that men should fear,
> Seeing that death, a necessary end,
> Will come when it will come.

The terminal state is also described in simple word portraits and brief descriptions.

> *Clifford.* Here burns my candle out; ay, here it dies, . . .
> > 3 *King Henry VI,* II, vi, 1

> *York.* Though death be poor, it ends a mortal woe.
> *King Richard.* The ripest fruit first falls . . .
> > *King Richard II,* II, i, 152

> *Shallow.* Death, as the Psalmist saith, is certain to all; all shall die.
> > 2 *King Henry IV,* III, ii, 36

> *Bardolph.* Well, the fuel is gone that maintain'd that fire; . . .
> > *King Henry V,* II, iii, 43

Death by strangulation is portrayed in the murder of Gloucester in 2 *King Henry VI.* The Earl of Warwick first

[169]

describes the appearances of a person who died by natural causes, and then contrasts that description with the appearance of the strangled Gloucester. Many of the modern medico-legal signs defining strangulation have been stated in this remarkable description (III, ii, 160):

> See how the blood is settled in his face.
> Oft have I seen a timely-parted[10] ghost,
> Of ashy semblance, meagre, pale and bloodless,
> Being all descended[11] to the labouring heart,
> Who, in the conflict that it holds with death,
> Attracts the same for aidance 'gainst the enemy,
> Which with the heart there cools, and ne'er returneth
> To blush and beautify the cheek again.

He then goes on to describe the signs of strangulation on the face of the victim (III, ii, 168-178):

> But see, his face is black and full of blood;
> His eye-balls further out than when he liv'd,
> Staring full ghastly like a strangled man;
> His hair uprear'd, his nostrils stretch'd with struggling;
> His hands abroad display'd, as one that grasp'd
> And tugg'd for life, and was by strength subdu'd.
> Look, on the sheets his hair, you see, is sticking;
> His well-proportion'd beard made rough and rugged,
> Like to the summer's corn by tempest lodged.[12]
> It cannot be but he was murd'red here:
> The least of all these signs were probable.

Death by drowning is also described, with emphasis on the environment rather than on the person (*King Richard III*, I, iv, 21):

> O Lord, methought what pain it was to drown,

What dreadful noise of waters in my ears,
What sights of ugly death within my eyes!
Methoughts I saw a thousand fearful wrecks,
A thousand men that fishes gnaw'd upon,
Wedges of gold, great anchors, heaps of pearl,
Inestimable stones, unvalued jewels,
All scatt'red in the bottom of the sea;
Some lay in dead men's skulls, and in those holes
Where eyes did once inhabit there were crept,
As 'twere in scorn of eyes, reflecting gems,
That woo'd the slimy bottom of the deep
And mock'd the dead bones that lay scatt'red by.

The difficulties of rescuing a drowning man when he clings
to his rescuer are described in few words (*Macbeth*, I, ii, 8):

Sergeant. As two spent swimmers that do cling together
And choke their art.

Death by poisoning was a frequent occurrence, both on
the stage and in real life. Hamlet's father and King John
were two of Shakespeare's most notable characters who met
an untimely end by poisoning. The ghost of Hamlet's father
relates the effects of poison on him – 'murder most foul' (I,
v, 64):

               ...whose effect
Holds such an enmity with blood of man
That swift as quicksilver it courses through
The natural gates and alleys of the body;
And with a sudden vigour it doth posset[13]
And curd, like eager[14] droppings into milk,
The thin and wholesome blood. So did it mine;...

Poisons exerted great fascination. They were derived

[171]

from plants, minerals, and many different sources. Some were considered medicinal – 'In poison there is physic' (2 *King Henry IV*, I, i, 137) – presumably in small doses, in much the same way as arsenic was used therapeutically until quite recently. Says Friar Lawrence (*Romeo and Juliet*, II, iii, 23):

Within the infant rind of this weak flower
Poison hath residence, and medicine power;
For this, being smelt, with that part cheers each part;
Being tasted, slays all senses with the heart.
Two such opposed kings encamp them still[15]
In man as well as herbs – grace[16] and rude will;[17]
And where the worser is predominant,
Full soon the canker death eats up that plant.

Iago (Othello, III, iii, 330) compares jealousy to a poison:

Dangerous conceits are[18] in their natures poisons
Which at the first are scarce found to distaste
But, with a little act upon the blood,
Burn like the mines of sulphur.

An early or impending death is described by many characters:

Richard. A deadly groan, like life and death's departing.
3 *King Henry VI*, II, vi, 43

Warwick: My mangled body shows,
My blood, my want of strength, my sick heart shows,
That I must yield my body to the earth.
3 *King Henry VI*, V, ii, 7

Ophelia. He rais'd a sigh so piteous and profound
As it did seem to shatter all his bulk
And end his being.
Hamlet, II, i, 94

Ellen Terry as Queen Katharine in *King Henry VIII*
(Act III, Scene I). From *The Complete Works of
William Shakespeare* (c. 1910). Photograph:
Window & Grove, London.

King. Ah, what a sign it is of evil life
Where death's approach is seen so terrible!

2 *King Henry VI,* III, iii, 5

King Edward. I every day expect an embassage[19]
From my Redeemer to redeem me hence;
And more at peace my soul shall part to heaven
Since I have made my friends at peace on earth.

King Richard III, II, i, 3

King John. For I do see the cruel pangs of death
Right in thine eye.

King John, V, iv, 59

Queen Katharine. My legs like loaden branches bow to th' earth,
Willing to leave their burden.

King Henry VIII, IV, ii, 2

The Duke of York (stabbed by his Queen):

Open Thy gate of mercy, gracious God!
My soul flies through these wounds to seek out Thee.

3 *King Henry VI,* I, iv, 177

John of Gaunt. My oil-dried lamp and time-bewasted light
Shall be extinct with age and endless night;
My inch of taper[20] will be burnt and done ...

King Richard II, I, iii, 221

And, again (*King Richard II,* II, i, 136):

Convey me to my bed, then to my grave.
Love they to live that love and honour have.

Hotspur. ... the earthy and cold hand of death
Lies on my tongue.

1 *King Henry IV,* V, iv, 84

Claudio, a young gentlemen (*Measure for Measure*, III, i, 84):

> If I must die
> I will encounter darkness[21] as a bride
> And hug it in mine arms.

Othello puts a nautical twist to the end of his journey (V, ii, 270):

> Here is my journey's end, and here is my butt,[22]
> And very sea-mark[23] of my utmost sail.[24]

A humble shepherd lives for the hour (*The Winter's Tale*, IV, iv, 453):

> If I might die within this hour, I have liv'd
> To die when I desire.

King Henry VI instructs his noblemen to carry out a post-mortem examination (2 *King Henry VI*, III, ii, 132):

> Enter his chamber, view his breathless corpse,
> And comment then upon his sudden death.

Shakespeare also mentions *rigor mortis* (*King John*, II, i, 352):

> *Bastard.* O, now doth Death line his dead chaps with steel; ...

Euthanasia has always been a controversial subject. In those days, as now, there have been special circumstances in which the continued existence of some unfortunate, suffering person has been questioned. King Richard has these unkind words to say of his dying old uncle, John of Gaunt (*King Richard II*, I, iv, 59):

> Now put it, God, in the physician's mind
> To help him to his grave immediately!

Come, gentlemen, let's all go visit him.
Pray God we may make haste, and come too late!

Hamlet was portrayed as a man who suffered from the effects of depression. Suicide is a complication of this illness, and Shakespeare had sufficient insight into the sufferings of a person with mental illness to portray accurately in Hamlet the association between depression and suicide. Hamlet's famous 'To be or not to be' soliloquy – in other words, 'To live or not to live' – represents a state in which he discusses with himself the act of self-destruction (*Hamlet*, III, i, 56). He reflects on what may happen after death: it may not be smooth sailing after all. Hamlet's father was tortured in purgatory for the foul crimes he had committed during his lifetime and reappeared on earth as a ghost! No wonder that men would prefer to endure the miseries and calamities of life rather than to escape by suicide, a sin which may result in unknown, and possibly worse, miseries in the next world:

To be, or not to be – that is the question;
Whether 'tis nobler in the mind to suffer
The slings and arrows of outrageous fortune,
Or to take arms against a sea[28] of troubles,
And by opposing end them? To die, to sleep –
No more; and by a sleep to say we end
The heart-ache and the thousand natural shocks
That flesh is heir to. 'Tis a consummation[26]
Devoutly to be wish'd. To die, to sleep;
To sleep, perchance to dream. Ay, there's the rub;[27]
For in that sleep of death what dreams may come,
When we have shuffled off this mortal coil,[28]
Must give us pause. There's the respect

The *Danse macabre,* an engraving by Hans Holbein the
Younger. The *danse macabre* was a popular subject
among artists in the Middle Ages. Photograph
from the Metropolitan Museum of Art, New York.

'The Dropsical Woman' by Gérard Dou (1613-1675).
(The Louvre, Paris.)

That makes calamity of so long life;[29]
For who would bear the whips and scorns of time,
Th' oppressor's wrong, the proud man's contumely,[30]
The pangs of despis'd love, the law's delay,
The insolence of office,[31] and the spurns
The patient merit of th' unworthy takes,[32]
When he himself might his quietus[33] make
With a bare bodkin?[34] Who would these fardels[35] bear,
To grunt and sweat under a weary life,
But that the dread of something after death –
The undiscover'd country, from whose bourn[36]
No traveller returns – puzzles the will,[37]
And makes us rather bear those ills we have
Than fly to others that we know not of?

Hamlet's fear of suicide* was enough to make him afraid of death and final judgement. He hesitates, because he has fears that are common to all (III, i, 84):

Thus conscience does make cowards of us all;
And thus the native hue of resolution[38]
Is sicklied o'er with the pale cast[39] of thought,
And enterprises of great pitch[40] and moment,
With this regard, their currents turn awry
And lose the name of action.[41]

Man will prefer to go on living, either because of human habit or because of the 'dread of something after death', the fear of the unknown. However, Cleopatra plans her suicide after the

---

*This was also expressed in another famous soliloquy: 'O that this too too solid flesh would melt, Thaw, and resolve itself into a dew!' (*Hamlet*, I, ii, 129) – which could, in another context, refer to his pangs of dieting!

[177]

Cleopatra (Peggy Ashcroft), Charmian (Jean
Wilson), and Iras (Mary Watson), in Act V, Scene
II, of a production of *Antony and Cleopatra* by the
Shakespeare Memorial Theatre in 1953.
Photograph by Angus McBean: reproduced by
courtesy of The Shakespeare Birthplace Trust.

[178]

death of her Antony (*Antony and Cleopatra*, IV, xv, 80):

> Then is it sin
> To rush into the secret house of death
> Ere death dare come to us?

Othello has similar motives when he suspects his wife's infidelity (III, iii, 390):

> I'll have some proof. Her name, that was as fresh
> As Dian's visage, is now begrim'd and black
> As mine own face. If there be cords or knives,
> Poison, or fire, or suffocating streams,
> I'll not endure it.

Menenius, a friend to Coriolanus, one of Shakespeare's bravest characters, was a renowned warrior, and the anticipation of death by his own hand was an expression of his own natural philosophy (*Coriolanus* V, ii, 100):

> He that hath a will to die by himself fears it not from another.

And so Shakespeare goes on from play to play, describing the death of his characters in most eloquent prose and majestic verse. Lest this morbid chapter be unduly prolonged (*Romeo and Juliet*, V, iii, 228):

> *Friar Lawrence.* I will be brief, for my short date of breath
> Is not so long as is a tedious tale.

Othello (Harry Andrews) and Desdemona
(Margaret Johnston), in Act III, Scene III, of a
production of *Othello* by the Shakespeare
Memorial Theatre in 1956. Photograph by Angus
McBean; reproduced by courtesy of The
Shakespeare Birthplace Trust.

13
THE
SPECIAL SENSES

Mercutio. Men's eyes were made to look,* and let them gaze.
Romeo and Juliet, III, i, 52

ANY REFERENCES of medical interest to the eyes, and to a lesser extent to the ears, occur in several plays; these reveal some remarkable powers of observation. For instance, it was expected that the eye of a king would resemble that of an eagle, and the faithful Duke of York says this about the eye of his King (*King Richard* II, III, iii, 68):

> Behold, his eye,
> As bright as is the eagle's, lightens forth
> Controlling majesty.

A shepherdess speaks to a shepherd (*As You Like It,* III, v, 11):

> 'Tis pretty, sure,[1] and very probable,
> That eyes, that are the frail'st and sofest things,
> Who shut their coward gate on atomies[2]
> Should be call'd tyrants, butchers, murderers!

---

*look: that is, at the opposite sex

[181]

Brutus tells Cassius (*Julius Caesar*, I, ii, 52):

> ... the eye sees not itself
> But by reflection, by some other things.

Says Prospero, the Duke of Milan (*The Tempest*, I, ii, 408):

> The fringed curtains of thine eye advance,[3]
> And say what thou seest yond.

Failing vision, a common symptom, is described by Edgar, the son of Gloucester, who had the miserable task of taking his blind father to the top of a cliff, and then, looking down, feels the effects of height on himself (*King Lear*, IV, vi, 22):

> I'll look no more;
> Lest my brain turn, and the deficient sight
> Topple down headlong.[4]

Again, Brutus cannot believe his eyes when he sees the ghost of Caesar (*Julius Caesar*, IV, iii, 274):

> I think it is the weakness of mine eyes
> That shapes this monstrous apparition.

Among his other problems of senility, Lear had failing vision (*King Lear*, V, iii, 279):

> Mine eyes are not o' th' best. I'll tell you straight.

Two common symptoms, itchy eyes and lachrymation, are described in few words (*Othello*, IV, iii, 56):

> *Desdemona.*   Mine eyes do itch;
> Doth that bode weeping?

And (*Timon of Athens*, I, ii, 102):

> *Timon.* Mine eyes cannot hold out water.

Lachrymation is again expressed in more elegant verse by
Capulet, speaking to his weepy daughter Juliet (*Romeo and
Juliet*, III, v, 129):

> What, still in tears?
> Evermore show'ring? In one little body
> Thou counterfeit'st[5] a bark,[6] a sea, a wind;
> For still thy eyes, which I may call the sea,
> Do ebb and flow with tears. The bark thy body is,
> Sailing in this salt flood; the winds thy sighs,
> Who, raging with thy tears, and they with them,
> Without a sudden calm will overset
> Thy tempest-tossed body.

Cataract is described as 'eyes blind with pin and web'
(*Winter's Tale*, I, ii, 290), and again in *King Lear* (III, iv, 113):
'This is the foul friend Flibbertigibbet ... he gives the web
and the pin, squenes the eye, and makes the hare-lip.' Many
signs and symptoms of other eye diseases are also mentioned. Diplopia – a 'parted eye' – for instance, affects Hermia in the fairyland of *A Midsummer Night's Dream* (IV, i,
186):

> Methinks I see these things with parted eye,
> When every thing seems double.

The fear of losing one's eyesight is expressed by the
young Arthur (*King John*, IV, i, 91):

> *Arthur.* Is there no remedy?
> *Hubert.*   None, but to lose your eyes.
> *Arthur.* O heaven, that there were but a mote[7] in yours,
> A grain, a dust, a gnat, a wandering hair,
> Any annoyance in that precious sense![8]

[183]

A popular belief was that the muscles or tendons of the eye ('eyestrings') were supposed to break when a man went blind. This was expressed by Imogen when she said (*Cymbeline*, I, iii, 17): 'I would have broke mine eyestrings, crack'd them ...'

There are descriptions of blindness in several plays. The most outstanding is in the famous words of the lovesick Romeo (*Romeo and Juliet*, I, i, 230):

> He that is strucken blind cannot forget
> The precious treasure of his eyesight lost.

Oberon says (*Midsummer Night's Dream*, III, ii, 369): 'And make his eyeballs roll with wonted sight.' With reference to Hamlet, walking around as if in a trance, Ophelia says (II, i, 98):

> He seem'd to find his way without his eyes;
> For out adoors he went without their helps ...

Edgar, sympathising with his blind father, says (*King Lear*, IV, vi, 5):

> ... your other senses grow imperfect
> By your eyes' anguish.

A jailer refers to blindness thus (*Cymbeline*, V, iv, 188):

> ... a man should have the best use of eyes to see the way of blindness!

Love, or Cupid, has traditionally always been blind. This is explained by Helena, very much in love with Demetrius, (*Midsummer Night's Dream*, I, i, 234):

> Love looks not with the eyes, but with the mind;

And therefore is wing'd Cupid painted blind.

A strange look in one's eye may reveal inward feelings, and this is expressed by Lennox *in Macbeth* (I, ii, 47):

What a haste looks through his eyes!
So should he look that seems to speak things strange.

The changed eyes of an old man are linked with other characteristics of age, and the ageing King Henry V speaks about himself (*King Henry V,* V, ii, 160):

A good leg will fall; a straight back will stoop; a black beard will turn white; a curl'd pate will grow bald; a fair face will wither; a full eye will wax hollow.

The signs of impending death may also be seen in the eyes (*King John,* V, iv, 59):

Salisbury. For I do see the cruel pangs of death
Right in thine eye.

Spectacles had been invented in about 1275, and were in rough use in the Elizabethan period. A piece of glass or a precious stone was not infrequently used as a magnifying glass, and this seems to be the allusion in Imogen's remark (*Cymbeline,* I, vi, 35):

Can we not
Partition make with spectacles so precious
'Twixt fair and foul?

A healthy interrelationship between vision and hearing is necessary for the adequate functioning of both organs. This is referred to in many plays, and the references demonstrate the remarkable links that Shakespeare created be-

tween these special senses. The mentally disturbed Hamlet
tells his mother (*Hamlet*, III, iv, 78):

> Eyes without feeling, feeling without sight,
> Ears without hands or eyes, smelling sans[9] all,
> Or but a sickly part of one true sense
> Could not so mope.[10]

To this she replies in similar vein (III, iv, 88):

> O Hamlet, speak no more!
> Thou turns't mine eyes into my very soul;
> And there I see such black and grained spots
> As will not leave their tinct.[11]

Also, Gloucester says (2 *King Henry VI*, III, i, 154): '... red
sparkling eyes blab his heart's malice.' King Richard speaks
to Mowbray (*King Richard II*, I, iii, 208):

> ... even in the glasses of thine eyes
> I see thy grieved heart.

A brief and remarkable description of reflex action and
the conditioned reflex between the eyes and nose is epito-
mised in four words (*All's Well that Ends Well*, V, iii, 314):
'Mine eyes smell onions.'

The sense of smell, which was probably severely taxed in
the streets of Shakespeare's London, has this description
(*Winter's Tale*, I, ii, 420):

> *Polixenes.* Turn then my freshest reputation to
> A savour[12] that may strike the dullest nostril
> Where I arrive, and my approach be shunn'd,
> Nay, hated too, worse than the great'st infection
> That e'er was heard or read!

The sense of hearing is not elaborated to the same extent

as vision. It is generally considered that hearing is more acute in darkness, and this belief is expressed by Hermia, whose amorous adventures took place at night (*Midsummer Night's Dream*, III, ii, 177):

> Dark night, that from the eye his function takes,
> The ear more quick of apprehension makes;
> Wherein it doth impair the seeing sense,
> It pays the hearing double recompense.

Helena suspects that Hermia, a close friend, is getting involved in her own love affair (I, i, 188):

> My ear should catch your voice, my eye your eye,
> My tongue should catch your tongue's sweet melody.

The lack of concentration and the inattention of old people are again referred to (*Love's Labour's Lost*, II, i, 74):

> *Rosaline*. ... aged ears play truant at his tales,
> And younger hearings are quite ravished.

Julius Caesar tells about his own deafness, presumably in his left ear. This disability, however, is not mentioned by any historian (*Julius Caesar*, I, ii, 213):

> Come on my right hand, for this ear is deaf,
> And tell me truly what thou think'st of him.

Disbelief is expressed when Miranda learns of her father's past (*The Tempest*, I, ii, 106): 'Your tale, sir, would cure deafness.'

And again in the same play (II, i, 100), the King of Naples speaks:

> You cram these words into mine ears against
> The stomach of my sense.

Friar Laurence (Max Adrian), in a production of
Romeo and Juliet by the Royal Shakespeare Theatre
in 1961. Photograph by Angus McBean; reproduced
by courtesy of The Shakespeare Birthplace Trust.

No better description of otitis externa (or otitis media) could be formulated than this given by Pisanio (*Cymbeline*, III, ii, 3): 'What a strange infection is fall'n into thy ear!' And (*Love's Labour's Lost*, V, ii, 851):

Rosaline. ... sickly ears,
Deaf'd with the clamours of their own dear groans ...

And finally, in a few terse words a remarkable description of these two organs (*Coriolanus*, II, i, 59):

Menenius. ... your bisson conspectuities ... *

And (*King Lear*, I, ii, 88):

Edmund. ... by an auricular assurance have your satisfaction.†

---

*Bleary-eyed vision.
†Proof that is heard with your own ears.

William Harvey (1578-1657), portrait by Rolls
Park in 1627. His proof of the circulation of the
blood within a closed system was the most
significant achievement in medicine and
physiology in the 17th Century. (Courtesy of the
National Portrait Gallery, London.)

14
THE 'SOVEREIGN THRONES'

Duke. ...liver, brain, and heart,
these sovereign thrones...
Twelfth Night, I, i, 37

HE MOST INTERESTING chapter in Renaissance physiology was probably that which was concerned with the circulation of the blood. This subject probably constituted the fulcrum of all physiological knowledge, and one cannot speak of true progress in physiology until the secrets of the circulation were revealed. Up to that time it was believed that the liver was the centre of the circulation, and hence the greatest importance was given to this organ. It was thought that the liver was the source of blood formation and 'heat generation'. An organ so large and vascular as the liver was necessarily supposed to have an important and intricate relationship with the blood. Moreover, psychological beliefs connected the liver, in a general way, with both courage and cowardice. Love and other emotions were also supposed to spring from the heat-generating properties of the liver, to add to its many loosely defined and widespread functions.

Wine had the effect of 'heating' the liver – no different from a similar belief which exists among some even today.

When the soothsayer says to Charmian, one of Cleopatra's attendants, 'You shall be more beloving than beloved', she sharply retorts: 'I had rather heat my liver with drinking' (*Anthony and Cleopatra*, I, ii, 22). The same effect of alchohol 'heating' the liver is implied when Gratiano speaks to his friend Antonio (*Merchant of Venice*, I, i, 81):

> And let my liver rather heat with wine
> Than my heart cool with mortifying groans.

Falstaff, one of Shakespeare's heavy drinkers, who was as much at ease in the presence of royalty as he was in a tavern or a drinking house, gives a glowing account of the virtues of his 'excellent sherris' (2 *King Henry IV,* IV, iii, 110):

> The second properties of your excellent sherris is the warming of the blood; which before, cold and settled, left the liver white and pale, which is the badge of pusillanimity and cowardice...

The absence of blood from the liver was thought to be a mark of cowardice and weakness. The connection between the liver and cowardice is again referred to by Bassanio in *The Merchant of Venice* (III, ii, 83):

> How many cowards, whose hearts are all as false
> As stairs of sand, wear yet upon their chins
> The beards of Hercules and frowning Mars;
> Who, inward search'd, have livers white as milk!

'Livers white as milk' — what a remarkable description of cowardice! Troilus, one of sons of the King of Troy, similarly says (*Troilius and Cressida*, II, ii, 49):

> Reason and respect
> Make livers pale and lustihood deject.

[192]

Examination of the patient: frontispiece of
Augusta's *Regimen sanitatis* (1482). For the
mediaeval physician the uroscope was a constant
reminder of his art. (From *A History of Medicine* by
A. Castiglioni, 1941.)

'Death and the Physician', by Hans Holbein
(1525). The picture shows the physician in his
laboratory, possibly counting his money, with death
looking at him over his shoulder. Reproduced by
permission of the British Library, London.

Kent calls Oswald (*King Lear*, II, ii, 16) 'lily-liver'd, action-taking, whoreson*...'. Macbeth says (V, iii, 15):

> Thou lily-liver'd boy...
> ...Those linen cheeks of thine
> Are counsellors to fear.

Love was also considered to be generated in the liver's heat. This was referred to by Ferdinand, son of the King of Naples (*The Tempest*, IV, i, 55):

> The white cold virgin snow upon my heart
> Abates the ardour of my liver.

Says Friar Francis (*Much Ado about Nothing*, IV, i, 230):

> Then shall he mourn,
> If ever love had interest in his liver.

On the other hand, temper and anger were also humours originating in the liver. Says Falstaff (2 *King Henry IV*, I, ii, 163):

> you do measure the heat of our livers with the bitterness of your galls;

And his companion Pistol has the courage to remark (V, v, 31):

> My knight, I will inflame thy noble liver
> And make thee rage.

---

*whoreson: son of a whore, a common slang expression. He continues his insult with: "...glass-gazing, superserviceable, finical rogue; one-trunk-inheriting slave,...a knave, beggar, coward, pander, and the son and heir of a mongrel bitch!"

Sir Toby Belch makes an unusual promise (*Twelfth Night*, III, ii, 58):

> For Andrew, if he were open'd, and you find so much blood in his liver as will clog the foot of a flea, I'll eat the rest of th' anatomy.

Shakespeare provided a remarkable description of the body's digestive functions by tracing the course of food in its passage through the body. Perhaps he was not technically correct in some respects, but at the same time he displayed remarkable insight into the body's functions (*Coriolanus*, I, i, 129):

> That I receive the general food at first
> Which you do live upon; and fit it is,
> Because I am the storehouse and the shop
> Of the whole body. But, if you do remember,
> I send it through the rivers of your blood,
> Even to the court, the heart, to th' seat o' th' brain;
> And, through the cranks[1] and offices[2] of man,
> The strongest nerves[3] and small inferior veins
> From me[4] receive that natural competency
> Whereby they live.

The second 'sovereign throne', the human brain, was then considered the seat of the soul and the source of intelligence and reasoning. The brain is also referred to several times. Strangely, in most of these references, one can almost sense a fear that some mishap or defective reasoning may affect this vital organ (*Othello*, IV, i, 266):

> *Lodovico.* Are his wits safe? Is he not light of brain?

And (*Macbeth*, I, iii, 149):

Macbeth. My dull brain was wrought
  With things forgotten.

Laertes, on seeing a mentally deranged Ophelia, says (*Hamlet,* IV, v, 151): 'O, heat dry up my brains!'

When Malvolio argues with the clown that he is not mad, the latter replies with pathological precision (*Twelfth Night,* IV, ii, 112): 'Nay, I'll ne'er believe a madman till I see his brains'.

The pia mater is mentioned on three occasions. In these two quotations one could not find a more polite description for calling a man stupid:

Clown... one of thy kin has a most weak pia mater.
Twelfth Night, I, v, 108
Thersites. I will buy nine sparrows for a penny, and his pia mater is not worth the ninth part of a sparrow.
Troilus and Cressida, II, i, 68

In a more elaborate description of higher intellectual function, the ventricles as well as the pia mater are discussed as the source of memory (*Love's Labour's Lost,* IV, ii, 62):

Holofernes. This is a gift that I have, simple, simple; a foolish extravagant spirit, full of forms, figures, shapes, objects, ideas, apprehensions, motions, revolutions. These are begot in the ventricle of memory, nourish'd in the womb of pia mater, and delivered upon the mellowing of occasion.

Polonius, the Lord Chamberlain in *Hamlet,* was worried about his own sanity when he stated (II, ii, 46):

...this brain of mine

Hunts not the trail of policy so sure
As it hath us'd to do.

The Elizabethan Age produced many explorers who sailed into uncharted seas and suffered great privations from lack of fresh food. Shakespeare compared the 'remainder biscuit', the dried biscuits left over at the end of a voyage, with a man's brain (*As You Like It*, II, vii, 38):

Jaques.   and in his brain,
Which is as dry as the remainder biscuit
After a voyage, he hath strange places cramm'd
With observation, the which he vents[5]
In mangled forms.[6]

Certainly, no brain could be drier than a 'remainder biscuit' at the end of an ocean voyage!

The most favourable situation is described briefly in *Antony and Cleopatra* (IV, viii, 21) as: 'A brain that nourishes our nerves...'

The third 'sovereign throne', the heart, was also frequently mentioned. According to Galenic medicine, the accepted physiological doctrine of the time, blood was supposed to be produced in the liver where it received 'natural spirit', and from this organ it flowed out to the periphery of the body by a pulling or atractive force, after having received 'animal spirits' in the brain and 'vital spirits' in the heart. Melancholic humour was considered to thicken and heat the heart's blood:

Romeo. Dry sorrow drinks our blood.

Romeo and Juliet, III, v, 59

King John. Or if that surly spirit, melancholy,
Hath bak'd thy blood and made it heavy-thick, . . .
King John, III, iii, 42

Messenger. Seeing too much sadness hath congeal'd your blood,
And melancholy is the nurse of frenzy.
Taming of the Shrew, Induction, ii,129

Sorrow, grief, joy and other emotions were part of the phenomenon of melancholic humour, and were also incorporated into the physiology of the heart:

Marcus. Sorrow concealed, like an oven stopp'd,
Doth burn the heart to cinders where it is.
Titus Andronicus, II, iv, 36

Westmoreland. My heart for anger burns; I cannot brook it.
3 *King Henry VI,* I, i, 60

Katherina. My tongue will tell the anger of my heart,
Or else my heart, concealing it, will break.
Taming of the Shrew, IV, iii, 77

Enobarbus.   Throw my heart
Against the flint and hardness of my fault,
Which, being dried with grief, will break to powder.
Antony and Cleopatra, IV, ix, 15

King John. The tackle[7] of my heart is crack'd and burnt,
And all the shrouds[8] wherewith my life should sail
Are turned to one thread, one little hair;
My heart hath one poor string to stay[9] it by,
Which holds but till thy news be uttered.
King John, V, vii, 52

In *Measure for Measure*, Angelo, contemplating the seduction of Isabella, exclaims (II, iv, 20):

> O heavens!
> Why does my blood thus muster to my heart,
> Making both it unable for itself,
> And dispossessing all my other parts
> Of necessary fitness?

When Portia expostulates with Brutus for not taking her into his confidence, he replies (*Julius Caesar*, II, i, 288):

> You are my true and honourable wife,
> As dear to me as are the ruddy drops
> That visit my sad heart.

'Swelling' of the heart was a favourite physiological state in the works of contemporary writers; they believed that it occurred whenever there was intense emotional activity, as in great anger or hate:

> *Gloucester.* The broken rancour of your high-swol'n hearts,
> But lately splintered, knit and join'd together.
> *King Richard III,* II, ii, 117

> *King Richard.* Swell'st thou, proud heart? I'll give thee scope to
> beat,
> Since foes have scope to beat both thee and me.
> *King Richard II,* III, iii, 140

> *Gloucester.* The King, thy sovereign, is not quite exempt
> From envious malice of thy swelling heart.
> 1 *King Henry VI,* III, i, 25

> *Coriolanus.* Measureless liar, thou has made my heart
> Too great for what contains it.
> *Coriolanus,* V, vi, 103

Aaron. Some devil whisper curses in my ear,
And prompt me that my tongue may utter forth
The venomous malice of my swelling heart!

> *Titus Andronicus,* V, iii, 11

Relief for the heart's anguish or swelling was obtained by weeping, sighing, groaning and so on, even though these activities 'consumed the life's blood'. They provided relief from the heart's 'passion', but if they were excessive, they became 'blood-consuming' or 'heart-offending':

Queen Margaret. Might liquid tears, or heart-offending groans,
Or blood-consuming sighs, recall his life,
I would be blind with weeping, sick with groans,
Look pale as primrose with blood-drinking sighs, ...

> 2 *King Henry VI,* III, ii, 60

Oberon. All fancy-sick she is and pale of cheer,
With sighs of love that costs the fresh blood dear.

> *Midsummer Night's Dream,* III, ii, 96

Queen Elizabeth. Ay, ay, for this I draw in many a tear
And stop the rising of blood-sucking sighs, ...

> 3 *King Henry VI,* IV, iv, 21

Troilus.   When my heart,
As wedged with a sigh, would rive in twain.

> *Troilus and Cressida,* I, i, 34

Othello is broken-hearted when he is told that his wife has been unfaithful, and in despair says (IV, i, 179):

No, my heart is turn'd to stone; I strike it, and it hurts my hand.

Likewise Hamlet's mother, also heartbroken at her son's unrepenting attitude towards her, says (III, iv, 156):

O Hamlet, thou has cleft my heart in twain.

The demented Lear, when faced with his daughter's ingratitude, says (II, iv, 284):

I have full cause of weeping; but this heart
Shall break into a hundred thousand flaws
Or ere I'll weep.

The circulation of the blood was discovered by William Harvey in 1628, sixteen years after Shakespeare's death. Up to this time the theories on the physiology of the human body considered the blood as being within the veins:

Hotspur. ... I'll empty all these veins[10]
And shed my dear blood drop by drop in the dust...
1 *King Henry IV,* I, iii, 133

Menenius. The veins unfill'd, our blood is cold, and then
We pout upon the morning, are unapt
To give or to forgive; but when we have stuff'd
These pipes and these conveyances of our blood...
Coriolanus, V, i, 51

Only the veins were believed to carry blood, and the arteries were considered to be a type of nervous system which had a relationship with vital spirits. Malvolio refers to an anatomical fact that blood returns from the surface of the extremities through the veins, when he says (*Twelfth Night,* III, iv, 20):

Sad, lady? I could be sad. This does make some obstruction in the blood, this cross-gartering...

The veins are mentioned over forty times in the plays, but

the arteries only twice. Their name* designates them as air-carriers, and they were also supposed to function as distributors and conveyors of the vital spirit:

> *Hamlet.* My fate cries out,
> And makes each petty artery in this body
> As hardy as the Nemean lion's nerve.†
>
> Hamlet, I, iv, 81

> *Berowne.* Why, universal plodding poisons up
> The nimble spirits[11] in the arteries,
> As motion and long-curing action tires
> The sinewy vigour of the traveller.
>
> Love's Labour's Lost, IV, iii, 301

Shakespeare originated many common expressions; among these was the idea of 'not liking the sight of blood' when he wrote (*As You Like It,* IV, iii, 157): 'Many will swoon when they do look on blood.'

Apart from the 'sovereign thrones', the liver, brain and heart, in Shakespeare's day there were, of course, other organs of vital significance. The spleen also had a complicated psysiological role. It was supposed to filter off the black choler and melancholic humour and to purify the body of these unwanted elements, thereby determining a person's disposition and temperament. Many emotions were consi-

---

*The word 'artery' (*arteria*) was used by early Greek physicians to describe the trachea and bronchi, because it was observed that they contained air and were empty after death. By the word 'veins' (*phlebes*) are meant those vessels which contain blood. The comparison between arteries, veins, nerves and tendons was elucidated many centuries later.

†The Nemean lion kept the people of the valley of Nemea in constant alarm. The first of the 12 labours of Hercules was to slay it. His club caused no impression on the lion, so he squeezed the beast to death.

---

dered to emanate from the spleen; sadness, anger, gaiety, envy and even lunacy were influenced by it. It is no wonder therefore that Shakespeare made many references to the spleen, and then carried these ideas further and elaborated on them.

In connection with happiness and laughter:

> *Maria.* If you desire the spleen, and will laugh yourself into stitches, follow me.
>> *Twelfth Night*, III, ii, 64

> *A Lord.* ... haply my presence
> May well abate the over-merry spleen.
>> *Taming of the Shrew*, Induction, i, 134

In connection with stupidity or madness:

> *Rosalind.* ....begot of thought, conceiv'd of spleen, and born of madness.
>> *As You Like It*, IV, i, 191

> *Worcester.* A hare-brain'd Hotspur, govern'd by a spleen.
> All his offences live upon my head...
>> 1 *King Henry IV*, V, ii, 19

In connection with courage:

> *Ulysses.* Or give me ribs of steel! I shall split all
> In pleasure of my spleen.
>> *Troilus and Cressida*, I, iii, 177

There are many more references to the spleen in which Shakespeare comments on the functions of this lesser-known organ in accordance with the current knowledge of the time.

The body is a complex structure, and it does not grow easier when each individual part is studied. Shakespeare ac-

Hamlet (Alan Howard) and Gertrude (Brenda Bruce), in a production of *Hamlet* by the Royal Shakespeare Theatre in 1970. Photograph from The Shakespeare Birthplace Trust, Shakespeare Centre Library.

quired a good working knowledge of its various parts which enabled him to make many references to it in his plays. He simplifies the human body in beautiful words:

> *Iago:* Our bodies are our gardens to the which our wills[12]
> are gardeners...
> > *Othello,* I, iii, 320

> *Viola:* Alas, our frailty is the cause, not we!
> For such as we are made of, such we be.
> > *Twelfth Night,* II, ii, 29

Santorio Santorio (born 1561) was a leader in his
field. He constructed thermometers, measured the
pulse rate, and conducted experiments in
physiology, including studies of the 'insensible
perspiration'. This engraving is by Piccini, and is
taken from Santorio's *Opera Omnia* (1600). (From
A History of Medicine by A. Castiglioni, 1941.)

15
CLINICAL
DESCRIPTIONS

HE FOREMOST among all scholar-physicians of the Renaissance period was Thomas Linacre (1460-1524), a Fellow of All Souls' College, Oxford. He studied medicine in Italy, where he also translated many original Greek manuscripts into English. By doing so, he recorded some of the theories of Hippocrates, Galen and Dioscorides in an up-to-date and critical manner, thereby freeing medical teaching from confusing mediaeval theories which had been based on ancient and inaccurate texts. In 1501 he was appointed Court Physician, and through King Henry VIII was able to obtain a Charter for the foundation of the Royal College of Physicians in 1518.

Medicine at this period was still firmly rooted in the humoral hypothesis. However, the winds of change were slowly moving physicians to classify and study diseases objectively and to establish therapy on a rational basis. The main ancillary aids to diagnosis were very limited; they were usually astrology and urinoscopy. The time was thus ripe for a breakthrough.

The surgeons were mostly less educated, 'un-Latined' men generally drawn from a lower social rank. They were

A busy outpatient department, showing surgical procedures on the
head, eye, leg, mouth, bladder and genitals. (From Galen's works,
Venetian edition, 1550; Collection Bertarelli, Milan.)

technical craftsmen, and in 1540, 22 years after the physicians, received a charter of incorporation which resulted in
the formation of the Barber-Surgeons' Company. This produced an improvement in technical education and surgical
skills, together with a rise in their status, but they were still
intellectually and socially inferior to the physicians. For this

[206]

reason, surgeons were often given the title 'Mr' rather than 'Dr', a custom which exists even today. Unlike the physicians, they were unable to obtain an academic degree which would mark them out from the large army of quacks, barbers, mountebanks and others who practised surgery – some with success, and most with handsome profit.

Internal medicine and general practice had yet to emerge as independent entities. The practice of medicine was restricted to Oxford and Cambridge graduates, but as these were few in number, the local apothecary practising from his shop was able to serve the medical needs of the neighbourhood. Medical practice therefore was a complex and empirical system of herb doctoring, charms, astrology and superstition, combined with the time-honoured procedures of blood-letting, purging, sweating and vomiting, which had been handed down from century to century. There is no doubt that a good portion of day-to-day doctoring – 'I bought an unction of a mountebank' (*Hamlet,* IV, vii, 141) – was carried out by barbers, quacks, itinerant empirics and 'wise women', of whom many were available.

The apothecaries had by now also become a reputable and organised body, eventually to receive their own charter. Although still a variety of grocer (one who sold goods by the 'gross'), the true apothecary was a member of the Grocers' Guild. Dispensing medicine was his major function, and when Romeo drank up a powerful medicine, he put his faith in the one who gave it to him: 'O true apothecary! Thy drugs are quick' (*Romeo and Juliet,* V, iii, 119). It was not till 1607, and mainly through the efforts of Sir Francis Bacon, that a separate charter was granted to the apothecaries.

Bacon's motivation for doing this was an intense dislike of physicians, whom he hoped to annoy. By the end of Elizabeth's reign, apothecaries had risen in social status and had become a reputable and prosperous body of men.

The religious orders of both sexes, not surprisingly, had favourable opportunities to try their hand at the practice of medicine, as superstition and religion played a large part in everyday life. Thus the Abbess, in *The Comedy of Errors*, replies to the persistent Adriana (V, i, 102):

> *Abbess.* Be patient; for I will not let him stir
> Till I have us'd the approved means I have,
> With wholesome syrups, drugs, and holy prayers,
> To make of him a formal man again.
> It is a branch and parcel of mine oath,
> A charitable duty of my order;
> Therefore depart, and leave him here with me.

Within this framework of the practice of medicine and surgery, Shakespeare made many astute and relevant observations. For instance, discussing the illness of Hamlet, Polonius remarks to Hamlet's mother (II, ii, 100):

> ... and now remains
> That we find out the cause of this effect;
> Or rather say the cause of this defect,
> For this effect defective comes by cause.

Says Caesar about Cassius (*Julius Caesar*, I, ii, 201):

> He reads much,
> He is a great observer, and he looks
> Quite through the deeds of men.

The supernatural was commonly invoked in the working

of drugs, as it also was in the causation of disease. The
heavenly bodies, in particular, exercised a controlling influence, and from this the whole 'science' of astrology has
evolved. Physicians implicitly believed in the effects of the
stars and planets on human health. Two examples are given
below. Says Timon (*Timon of Athens*, IV, iii, 108):

> Be as a planetary plague, when Jove
> Will o'er some high-vic'd city hang his poison
> In the sick air; let not thy sword skip one.

And in *Troilus and Cressida* Ulysses says (I, iii, 89):

> And therefore is the glorious planet Sol
> In noble eminence enthron'd, and spher'd
> Amidst the other, whose med'cinable eye
> Corrects the ill aspects of planets evil,
> And posts, like the commandment of a king,
> Sans check, to good and bad. But when the planets
> In evil mixture to disorder wander,
> What plagues and what portents ...

There was no such thing as 'pathology'. One method of
assisting his clinical judgement which was available to a doctor was an age-old medical practice of diagnosing diseases
by 'water casting' or inspection of the patient's urine. Many
elderly patients will, to this day, bring a 'specimen' along
when they visit their doctor. Shakespeare refers to the practice of inspection of the urine on various occasions (2 *King
Henry IV*, I, ii, 1):

> *Falstaff*. ... what says the doctor to my water?
> *Page:* He said, sir, the water itself was a good healthy water;
> but for the party that owed it,[1] he might have moe[2] diseases
> than he knew for.

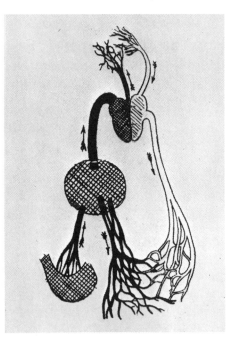

Galen's theory of the circulation of the
blood. Galen (c. 120-c. 200) wrote on a
number of medical subjects, and for nearly
1500 years his works remained standard
references (From *A History of Medicine*
by A. Castiglioni, 1941.)

In earlier days, clergy were often involved in the treatment of patients, but this practice was opposed by physicians, and an attempt was made to prohibit it, as the financial
rewards were considered detrimental to their piety. However,
the clergy overcame this simple problem by having the patient's urine brought to them and then suggesting treatment.
This practice soon became widespread, and any 'wise' person could diagnose by inspection of the urine. When Malvo-

lio is pronounced mad, Fabian says 'Carry his water to th' wise woman' (*Twelfth Night*, III, iv, 97):

With virtually no aids to diagnosis available, an astute physician would allow his imagination to soar when examining a patient's urine:

> *Macbeth*. If thou couldst, doctor, cast[3]
> The water of my land, find her disease,
> And purge it to a sound and pristine[4] health,
> I would applaud thee to the very echo.
>
> > *Macbeth*, V, iii, 50

And:

> *Speed*. … these follies are within you, and shine through you like the water in an urinal, that not an eye sees you but is a physician to comment on your malady.
>
> > *Two Gentlemen of Verona*, II, i, 34

To heap ridicule upon Dr Caius, in *The Merry Wives of Windsor*, the host thus accosts him (II, iii, 30): 'Thou art a Castalion-King Urinal.'* And soon after (II, iii, 51): 'A word, Mounseur Mockwater.'† And again, (III, i, 13), Evans threatens: 'I will knog his urinals about his knave's costard.'‡

These epithets are applied in jest, and probably indicate that Shakespeare, and many others, had come to ridicule the practice of urine casting, seeing what a shallow and unreliable practice it was. 'Water casting', however, was a major

---

* 'Castalion-King-Urinal' is a king-size in chamberpots.
† 'Mockwater' is one who misinterprets the signs in urine.
‡ 'costard' is a slang word for head, but literally means an apple.

preoccupation of the physician, and the urine flask became his pictorial symbol, much as the stethoscope is today. It was a favourite theme of painters and engravers, and the urinal, 'which should represent the bladder of man', was wide-mouthed and often divided into superior, middle and inferior zones which were related to comparable parts of the body. The urine was carefully examined as to colour, density and content, and the different kinds of clouds or precipitates that form on standing were observed. These aided in the deduction of the most important and far-reaching conclusions! Though the method had no diagnostic value, it held its position for centuries until displaced by the realistic and better-educated Renaissance doctors.

A simple illness, such as diarrhoea, must have been quite a scourge, and invariably would have to take its course before the patient got better. In a public place in Rome, Menenius teases two tribunes about their enmity towards Coriolanus now that he is coming home in honour. He compares them to a man suffering from diarrhoea, using unusual metaphors, perhaps not to offend them (*Coriolanus*, i, 67):

> ... if you chance to be pinch'd with the colic, you make faces like mummers,[5] set up the bloody flat against[6] all patience, and, in roaring for a chamber-pot, dismiss the controversy bleeding[7] ...

Another common symptom, loss of weight, is mentioned by Falstaff, but one suspects that he was merely asking his companion Bardolph for sympathy, as he had a lot of bulk to lose (1 *King Henry IV*, III, iii, 1):

> Bardolph, am I not fall'n away vilely since this last action? Do I not bate?[8] Do I not dwindle? Why, my skin hangs about me

like an old lady's loose gown; I am withered like an old apple-john.

Shakespeare's unique use of words described many common symptoms in a manner which today's medical experts would willingly use in textbooks of medicine. Take, for instance, his description of vertigo:

He that is giddy thinks the world turns round.
Taming of the Shrew, V, ii, 20

Turn giddy, and be holp⁹ by backward turning.
Romeo and Juliet, I, ii, 47

My thoughts are whirled like a potter's wheel;
I know not where I am nor what I do.
1 *King Henry VI*, I, v, 19

Anaemia was a serious problem, its cause as well as its treatment being still unknown. Shakespeare described it as follows (*Midsummer Night's Dream*, I, i, 128):

Lysander.   Why is your cheek so pale?
How chance the roses there do fade so fast?

Measurement of the pulse rate is a simple, everyday procedure; yet this became possibly only after a minute hand was added to the clock in the 1700s. Up to this time, physicians carefully palpated and examined the quality of the pulse even though they had no means of measuring its rate.*

---

*Santorio Santorio (1561-1636), an Italian physician, in 1602 devised an instrument called a 'pulsilagram' for measuring pulse rate. It consisted of a simple pendulum; the length of the suspended string was adjusted until the beat of the pendulum coincided with the pulse. He then measured the length of the pendulum.

Shakespeare refers several times to the human pulse, in health as well as in sickness:

Hamlet. My pulse as yours doth temperately keep time,
And makes as healthful music.

Hamlet, III, iv, 140

Troilus. My heart beats thicker than a feverous pulse ...

Troilus and Cressida, III, ii, 35

Pinch. Give me your hand, and let me feel your pulse.
Antipholus. There is my hand, and let it feel your ear.

Comedy of Errors, IV, iv, 49

Pericles.   But are you flesh and blood?
Have you a working pulse ...

Pericles, V, i, 151

King John. Have I commandment on the pulse of life?

King John, IV, ii, 92

Associated with examination of the pulse was observation of the heart's action. On this topic, and on palpitation, Shakespeare also had many comments:

Titus. Thou map of woe,[10] that thus dost talk in signs!
When thy poor heart beats with outrageous beating,
Thou canst not strike it thus to make it still.

Titus Andronicus, III, ii, 12

Leontes. I have tremor cordis on me; my heart dances,
But not for joy, not joy.

The Winter's Tale, I, ii, 110

Hamlet. Sir, in my heart there was a kind of fighting
That would not let me sleep.

Hamlet, V, ii, 4

The wild beating of the heart under a tightly laced corset of whalebone would certainly cause discomfort (*The Winter's Tale*, III, ii, 174):

Paulina. O, cut my lace, lest my heart, cracking it,
Break too!

In another place, in one of his long poems, Shakespeare gives an accurate description of palpitation attending nervous excitement – a not uncommon modern-day syndrome:

His hand, that yet remains upon her breast –
Rude ram, to batter such an ivory wall! –
May feel her heart, poor citizen, distress'd,
Wounding itself to death, rise up and fall,
Beating her bulk, that his hand shakes withal.

The Rape of Lucrece, 463

Breathlessness was a symptom which could not escape any observer, as the lack of breath made one ' ... almost dead for breath' (*Macbeth*, I, v, 33). Shakespeare made many references to dyspnoea:

York. 'Tis breath thou lack'st, and that breath wilt thou lose.

King Richard II, II, i, 30

Troilus. ... the birth of our own labouring breath.

Troilus and Cressida, IV, iv, 37

Ajax. Now crack thy lungs and split thy brazen pipe; ...
Come, stretch thy chest, and let thy eyes spout blood ...

Troilus and Cressida, IV, v, 7

And an obvious statement of fact:

Juliet: How art thou out of breath, when thou hast breath
To say to me that thou art out of breath?

Romeo and Juliet, II, v, 31

Until recent years, 'consumption' was synonymous with pulmonary tuberculosis. Earlier, it was used to describe cachectic states and general debility. The word 'consumption' is used at least twice in this sense:

> *Beatrice.* I would not deny you; but, by this good day, I yield upon great persuasion; and partly to save your life, for I was told you were in consumption.
>
> *Much Ado about Nothing* V, iv, 94

She evidently thinks the disease curable; not so Falstaff:

> *Falstaff.* I can get no remedy against this consumption of the purse; borrowing only lingers and lingers it out, but the disease is incurable.
>
> *2 King Henry IV,* I, ii, 222

Shakespeare mentions jaundice as a symptom based on the theory of bodily humours. Gratiano attempts to cheer up his friend Antonio, the Merchant of Venice, by telling him (I, i, 83):

> Why should a man whose blood is warm within
> Sit like his grandsire cut in alabaster,*
> Sleep when he wakes, and creep into the jaundice
> By being peevish?

And again we read:

> *Agamemnon.* What grief hath set these jaundies o'er your cheeks?
>
> *Troilus and Cressida,* I, iii, 1

---

*grandsire cut in alabaster: he refers to the alabaster image of his grandfather, alabaster being used for monuments and graves in churchyards.

Interior of the Hôtel – Dieu, Paris, one of the great hospitals of
Europe. The engraving shows the crowded conditions, and corpses
being sewn into their shrouds in full view of the other patients (From
MS. Ea. 17. rés., courtesy of Bibliothèque Nationale, Paris.)

'Lies crafty-sick' (2 *King Henry IV*, Induction, 37) – what a
perfect description for a malingerer! This 'illness' existed in
those days too. Timon was suspected of malingering by one
of his servants – 'he's much out of health and keeps his
chamber'; and another replies: 'Many do keep their chambers are not sick' (*Timon of Athens*, III, iv, 72).

The medical history of Falstaff, one of Shakespeare's

[217]

best-known characters, has sufficient material for a sixteenth century clinico-pathological conference. In one single scene (2 *King Henry IV,* I, ii, 2), the dialogue between Falstaff and his companion provides a variety of medical expressions. Falstaff asks his page:

> *Falstaff.* Sirrah, you giant, what says the doctor to my water?[11]
> *Page.* He said, sir, the water itself was a good healthy water; but for the party that owed[12] it, he might have moe diseases than he knew for.

Falstaff is a crafty fellow, and pretends not to hear the words of the Chief Justice:

> *Servant.* Sir John Falstaff!
> *Falstaff.* Boy, tell I am deaf.
> *Page.* You must speak louder; my master is deaf.
> *Chief Justice.* I am sure he is, to the hearing of anything good.

Falstaff then attempts to give good advice to the Chief Justice about his health:

> *Falstaff.* Your lordship, though not clean past your youth, hath yet some smack[13] of age in you, some relish of the saltness[14] of time, and I most humbly beseech your lordship to have a reverend care of your health.

Falstaff makes a fool of the Chief Justice by implying that he suffers from some type of fits:

> *Falstaff.* This apoplexy, as I take it, is a kind of lethargy ... a kind of sleeping in the blood, a whoreson tingling.
> *Chief Justice.* What tell you me of it? Be it as it is.
> *Falstaff.* It hath its original from much grief, from study, and perturbation of the brain. I have read the cause of his effects in Galen.[15] It is a kind of deafness.

Chief Justice. I think you are fall'n into the disease ...
Falstaff. ... it is the disease of not listening, the malady of not marking, that I am troubled withal.
Chief Justice. To punish you by the heels[16] would amend the attention of your ears; and I care not if I do become your physician.

In the same dialogue, the Chief Justice rebukes Falstaff, rubbing in the degenerative effects of age on 'this muddy vesture of decay':

Chief Justice. Well, I am loath to gall[17] a new-heal'd wound.
Falstaff. You that are old consider not the capacities of us that are young; you do measure the heat of our livers with the bitterness of your galls; and we that are in the vaward[18] of our youth, I must confess, are wags[19] too.
Chief Justice. Do you set down your names in the scroll of youth, that are written down old with all the characters[20] of age? Have you not a moist eye, a dry hand, a yellow cheek, a white beard, a decreasing leg, an increasing belly? Is not your voice broken, your wind short, your chin double, your wit single,[21] and every part of you blasted with antiquity? And will you yet call yourself young? Fie, fie, fie, Sir John!
Falstaff. A man can no more separate age and covetousness than 'a can part young limbs and lechery; But the gout galls the one and the pox pinches the other; and so both the degrees[22] prevent[23] my curses. Boy!

Falstaff is against fighting on a hot day, and wishes he may 'never spit white again'. The colour of the spittle was an important point in diagnosis, especially of temperament. To 'spit white' was possibly a sign that a man had drunk well, or 'spit clean', a sign of good health. Finally Falstaff, heavy, overweight and a big drinker, is affected by an attack of acute gout:

> *Falstaff*. A pox of this gout! or, a gout of this pox! for the one or the other plays the rogue with my great toe ... I will turn diseases to commodity.[24]

The state of the countenance which immediately precedes death, especially from acute infectious diseases, is the so-called 'Hippocratic facies', after Hippocrates who first described it: nose sharp, eyes hollow, temples sunken, ears cold and contracted with their lobes turned outwards, the skin about the face hard, tense, and dry, the colour of the face yellow or dark. This description has been repeated for generations in medical textbooks, and Shakespeare employed it to describe the death of Falstaff, who dominated the two plays about King Henry IV. His death was reported in *King Henry V* by the hostess of the Boar's Head Tavern, one of his frequent haunts (II, iii, 15):

> ... for after I saw him fumble with the sheets, and play with flowers, and smile upon his fingers' end, I knew there was but one way; for his nose was as sharp as a pen, and 'a babbl'd of green fields.
> ... I put my hand into the bed and felt them, and they were as cold as any stone; then I felt to his knees, and so upward and upward, and all was as cold as any stone.
> *Bardolph*. Well, the fuel is gone that maintain'd that fire.

Proceeding into the intricacies of clinical examination, Shakespeare recorded a unique observation – what appears today as a reference to examination of the central nervous system. This was made by Lear when he expressed this dread: 'I fear I am not in my perfect mind'; for he was far advanced in cerebral dementia (IV, vii, 54):

> I know not what to say.
> I will not swear these are my hands. Let's see.
> I feel this pin prick. Would I were assur'd
> Of my condition!

Even more remarkable was a reference to examination of the 'head' or brain, using the term 'scanned', which has now crept into the language of everyday clinical examination, although with a new meaning:

> *Macbeth*. Strange things I have in head that will to hand,
> Which must be acted ere they may be scann'd.[25]
>
> *Macbeth*, III, iv, 139

Title-page woodcut of *De humani corporis fabrica* (1543) by Andreas
Vesalius (1514-1564). He was the greatest anatomist of his day, and his
masterpiece, the *Fabrica,* was created with artistic details. Vesalius is
here seen giving an anatomy lecture. He is the dissector, unusual in
those days, Vesalius specifically mentioned the use of hands while
dissecting, which he said had been 'completely neglected by physicians
since the time of the Romans, because physicians left the manual work
to the others, and they lost their practical acquaintance with anatomy.'
Reproduced from *Medicine and the Artist (Ars Medica)* by permission of
the Philadelphia Museum of Art; Dover Publications, Inc., New York.

[222]

16
VARIOUS
DISEASES

EDICAL SCIENCE has advanced so considerably in the last few decades that it is now difficult to imagine what life was like even at the beginning of our own century. Diseases now unknown were then rife, and how much more precarious was the state of life in the fifteenth and sixteenth centuries! Going back a little into history, before Harvey described the circulation of blood, the general belief was that blood flowed back and forth in the body, like the ebb and flow of ocean tides. Although Harvey accurately demonstrated the circulation of blood, he still did not know how the arteries and veins were connected, and was unable to explain how blood would flow from one vascular system to the other. This discovery was achieved by an Italian physician, Marcello Malpighi, who was born in the year in which Harvey's work on the circulation was published. The opposition to new doctrine was so bitter that Harvey's first publication, *Movement of the Heart and Blood in Animals: An Anatomical Eassay,* was not published in England, but appeared in Frankfurt in 1628. In 1661, four years after Harvey's death, Malpighi showed that capillaries provided the connection between arteries and veins. In the 1600s

smallpox vaccination had not arrived, antisepsis was un-known, and the microscope was just being used for new discoveries. Those were the days of the renaissance of medicine, as of art, when such famous men as Vesalius Fallopius and Valsalva had begun scientific study of the cadaver.

In this context, diseases as we know them today were frequently described as a loose collection of symptoms and, of course, as the effects of imbalance of the 'humours'. So long as this doctrine held sway, different manifestations of disease were considered the result of humoral imbalance, and there appeared no reason to describe separate syn-dromes. Hence, many diseases which crop up in the plays are unnamed and merely called a 'sickness', a 'distemper' or an 'illness', and those which are named are spoken of in the common terms of ordinary lay language. Thus we also read of agues, scurvy, scald, gout, greensickness, hare-lip and so on. It was not till the 'great pox', syphilis, swept across Europe at the beginning of the sixteenth century, that physicians attempted to classify signs and symptoms into various disease entities in the modern sense.

However, the association between cause and effect had shown itself in some diseases; for instance, the bite of a rabid dog could produce a fatal illness. Shakespeare be-lieved, in common with others, that the venomous tooth of the dog caused the disease (*King Richard III*, I, iii, 289):

> ... take heed of yonder dog!
> Look when he fawns, he bites; and when he bites,
> His venom tooth will rankle[1] to the death:
> Have not to do with him, beware of him;
> Sin, death, and hell, have set their marks on him ...

Sick-bed scene; the religious orders, then as now, contributed much to the treatment of patients in hospitals. Woodcut from Boethius, *De consolatione philosophiae* (Lyons, 1498). (Courtesy of the Wellcome Institute Library, London.)

Plague was one of the commonest and most dreaded diseases of the time. The term 'Black Death' was first used in the seventeenth century to describe the appearance of the body after death, when haemorrhages under the skin gave the corpse a dark, mottled hue. Plague was endemic in London from 1590 to 1665. It was no stranger to the English capital, where the closely-packed, timbered houses harboured the black rat. In the absence of sanitation and drainage, householders threw their garbage and rubbish into the streets to await the 'rakers', who periodically cleared it away to the outskirts of the city. Plague caused over 33 000 deaths in London in 1603. Afflicted houses were quarantined and painted with a red cross and the words 'Lord have mercy on us', to warn passers-by to keep away:

> *Berowne.* Write 'Lord have mercy on us' on those three;
> They are infected; in their hearts it lies;
> They have the plague, and caught it of your eyes.
>
> *Love's Labour's Lost,* V, ii, 419

When a reddish petechial rash developed in a plague victim, the patient was usually well on his way to a fatal outcome:

> *Ulysses.* He is so plaguy proud that the death tokens[2] of it
> Cry 'No recovery'.
>
> *Troilus and Cressida,* II, iii, 172

> *Scarus.* On our side like the token'd pestilence,[2]
> Where death is sure.
>
> *Antony and Cleopatra,* III, x, 9

> *Volumnia.* Now the red pestilence strike all trades in Rome,
> And occupations perish!
>
> *Coriolanus,* IV, i, 13

The plague. Epidemics of plague repeatedly devastated large
populations in cities. The white space (top left) originally contained
Sebastian and Roch, the patron saints of plague victims. (From
Francesco Petrarca, *Von der Artzney Bayder Glück*, 1532.)

The horror of the disease was sufficient to cause it to be
considered as an agent of God's punishment:

Volumnia. . . . th' hoarded plague o' th' gods.

Coriolanus, IV, ii, 11

Various theories were proposed as to the cause of this
terrible scourge. Some believed that it came from a poisonous substance in the air or from wells, while others saw

plague as a mixture of planetary influences and divine vengeance.

An early attempt at quarantining plague victims was made in 1518 by the Mayor of Oxford, who ordered infected persons to stay within their houses for forty days. This order was based on earlier Italian methods of containing the disease, including keeping suspected travellers or carriers in a place distant from the harbour or city for thirty days. Soon, when it appeared that thirty days was not sufficient, the period was extended to forty days – a *quarantenaria* – from which our word 'quarantine' was derived. Special officials called 'searchers' were appointed, whose duty it was to go into houses and search out plague victims. They were paid a higher rate if the victims were found dead. The use of the word 'searcher' in this sense appeared in 1592 in *Romeo and Juliet*. Friar John, suspected of being in an infected house, was shut in by the 'searchers', and was thus prevented from carrying the all-important message from Friar Lawrence to Romeo. No messenger could be found to return the letter to Friar Lawrence, so afraid were the citizens of Verona of the infection (V, ii, 8):

> *Friar John.* And finding him, the searchers of the town,
> Suspecting that we both were in a house
> Where the infectious pestilence did reign,
> Seal'd up the doors, and would not let us forth ...

Another feared disease, leprosy, which was common in England in the Middle Ages (sixth to seventh centuries), was from the earliest times regarded as highly contagious. The mediaeval treatment of lepers is one of the dark examples of man's inhumanity. Lepers were believed to have transgressed against God, and were therefore isolated from the community. They were often banished from society and rigorously segregated from others:

> Queen Margaret. What, dost thou turn away, and hide thy face?
> I am no loathsome leper – look on me.
>
> 2 King Henry VI, III, ii, 74

The word 'leprosy' and 'lazar' are used many times. Probably there was no understanding of this disease, like many others, as a clinical entity. However, the contagious nature of the disease is recognised (*Timon of Athens*, IV, iii, 358):

> Timon. All villains that do stand by thee are pure.
> Apemantus. There is no leprosy but what thou speak'st.
> Timon. If I name thee.
> I'll beat thee – but I should infect my hands.

Plague and leprosy were not the only terrors. A new disease, the 'sweating sickness', first appeared in England as a severe epidemic in 1485. 'As it found them, so it took them; some in sleep, some in wake, some in mirth, some in care, some fasting, and some full, some busy and some idle.' Four more epidemics followed, and then, after the last in 1578, the disease disappeared. John Caius, founder of Caius College, Cambridge, wrote the first book in the English language on this mysterious disease, giving detailed observations in 'A boke, or counseill against the disease commonly called the sweats, or sweatynge sicknesse'. He recorded that the illness started with a sweat and fever. It was diagnosed by pains in the back and shoulder; then pains in the liver and stomach; 'thirdly by the pain in the head and madness (i.e. delirium)

Plague, the grim reaper; plague was often
considered a visitation from God as a punishment
for sins. Woodcut title page from Culmacher's
plague tract (c. 1495). (Courtesy of the Wellcome
Institute Library, London.)

of the same; fourthly by the passion (i.e. palpitation) of the heart.' Shakespeare dwelt on this mysterious 'ague' many times; King John was portrayed as a sufferer (*King John*, V, iii, 14):

> ... this tyrant fever burns me up
> And will not let me welcome this good news.
> ... to my litter straight;
> Weakness possesseth me, and I am faint.

Another victim was Salarino, a friend of Antonio, the Merchant of Venice (I, i, 22):

> My wind, cooling my broth,
> Would blow me to an ague ...

Malaria was, till recent times, a disease of temperate as well as of tropical countries. The word 'malaria' comes from two Italian words that mean 'bad air', because of its association with the musty, bad-smelling air of swamps. The commencement of spring, the month of March in the Northern Hemisphere, initiated outbreaks of malaria.

> *Hotspur.* ... worse than the sun in March,
> This praise doth nourish agues.
>
> 1 *King Henry IV*, IV, i, 111

Shakespeare was aware of the recurring nature of malaria. A fever which recurs daily is now called 'quotidian', and that which recurs every other day is 'tertian'. The final illness of Falstaff was of this nature (*King Henry V*, II, i, 116):

> *Hostess.* He is so shak'd of a burning quotidian tertian that it is most lamentable to behold.

A French physician, Guillaume de Baillou (1536-1616), in

[231]

his *'Liber de rheumatismo'*, was the first to use the word 'rheumatism' in the modern sense. He was, moreover, the first since Hippocratic times to distinguish between rheumatism and gout. This differentiation was also taken up by Shakespeare, who described the viciousness of acute gout in the obese Falstaff. When gout is confused with the 'pox', one wonders whether the syphilis of those days produced severe joint involvement or whether arthritis was misdiagnosed as a syphlitic sequel (2 *King Henry IV*, I, ii, 232):

> *Falstaff.* A pox of this gout! or, a gout of this pox! for the one or the other plays the rogue with my great toe.

That no effective remedy existed for the treatment of gout is proved by the following reference to gout as incurable (*Cymbeline*, V, iv, 4):

> *Posthumus.*   Yet am I better
> Than one that's sick o' th' gout, since he had rather
> Groan so in perpetuity than be cur'd
> By th' sure physician death, who is the key
> T' unbar these locks.

A common belief, which still persists today, is that there is a relationship between rheumatism and damp climatic conditions. This is expressed by Titania, the Queen of the Fairies, in the magical woods of *A Midsummer Night's Dream* (II, i, 88, 103):

> Therefore the winds, ...
>   ... have suck'd up from the sea
> Contagious fogs; ...

> Therefore the moon, the governess of floods,
> Pale in her anger, washes all the air,
> That rheumatic diseases do abound.

Plague fighter. This protective garb was developed
in the Middle Ages for doctors to wear when
plague was rampant. The 'beak' contained
pleasant-smelling substances to mitigate the evil
odours inevitably encountered.

Galen, between Hippocrates and Avicenna, the 'greats' of medical antiquity. Galen looked back to Hippocrates as his authority, and Avicenna looked to Galen for his knowledge.

(From an edition of the works of Galen
published in Lyons in 1528; courtesy of the
National Library of Medicine, Bethesda.)

'The Rat Killer', an etching by Jan Georg van Vliet.
The connection between rats and outbreaks of plague
had been known since biblical times. The rat killer
performed a valuable public health service.
(Courtesy of the National Library of Medicine, Bethesda.)

Shakespeare's description of arthritis, 'fever-weak'ned joints, like strengthless hinges' (Northumberland in 2 *King Henry IV*, I, i, 140) cannot be improved upon by any rheumatologist. Shakespeare frequently described the aches and pains of rheumatism, the stiff joints, the loss of mobility and other common symptoms:

Hamlet. ... my sinews, grow not instant old,
But bear me stiffly up.

> *Hamlet*, I, v, 94

Prospero. Fill all thy bones with aches, make thee roar ...

> *The Tempest*, I, ii, 370

Nurse. I am aweary, give me leave a while;
Fie, how my bones ache! What a jaunce have I had.

> *Romeo and Juliet*, II, v, 25

Desdemona. For let our finger ache, and it endues
Our other healthful members even to a sense
Of pain.

> *Othello,* III, iv, 147

Apemantus. Aches contract and starve your supple joints!

> *Timon of Athens,* I, i, 250

Gonzalo. My old bones ache.

> *The Tempest,* III iii, 2

Shakespeare may have been thinking of advanced kyphosis in an old woman when he wrote (*The Tempest*, I, ii, 258):

Prospero. The foul witch Sycorax, who with age and envy
Was grown into a hoop.

The term 'sciatica' was also used for arthritic afflictions, particularly of the lower extremities:

Timon. Thou cold sciatica

Cripple our senators, that their limbs may halt
As lamely as their manners.

Timon of Athens, IV, i, 23

1 Gentleman. How now! which of your hips has the most profound sciatica?

Measure for Measure, I, ii, 56

However, Shakespeare did make a joke of stiff joints – certainly an elephant does appear to meander in an arthritic
manner:

The elephant hath joints, but none for courtesy; his legs are
legs for necessity, not for flexure.

Troilus and Cressida, II, iii, 101

A huge goitre ('dew-lapp'd like bulls') was probably referred to when in *The Tempest* we read (III, iii, 43):

Gonzalo.   When we were boys,
Who would believe that there were mountaineers,
Dewlapp'd like bulls, whose throats had hanging at 'em
Wallets of flesh?

'Cramps' was used to define a loose variety of symptoms,
not necessarily confined to the extremities. Prospero curses
the deformed Caliban with a 'stitch in the side' which will
stop his breath (*The Tempest,* I, ii, 325):

For this, be sure, tonight thou shalt have cramps,
Side-stitches that shall pen thy breath up ...

Anorexia nervosa, essentially a disorder of hysterical
young women, was described as 'green sickness', a form of
anaemia common to teenage girls (*Antony and Cleopatra,* III,
ii, 5): ' ... is troubled with the green sickness.' Also, a similar

[234]

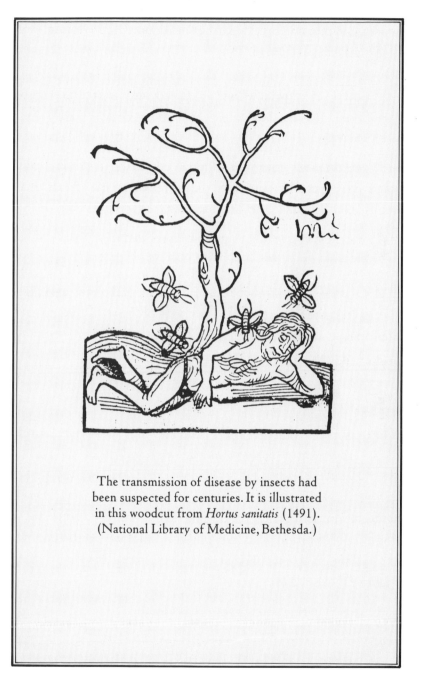

The transmission of disease by insects had
been suspected for centuries. It is illustrated
in this woodcut from *Hortus sanitatis* (1491).
(National Library of Medicine, Bethesda.)

anaemic syndrome was described as occurring in young men
(2 *King Henry IV,* IV, iii, 97):

> *Falstaff.* There's never none of these demure boys come to any
> proof; for thin drink doth so over-cool their blood, and mak-
> ing many fish-meals, that they fall into a kind of male green-
> sickness; ...

An extremely common clinical condition of today, cold
sores or herpes labialis, was then known as the 'Mab'. It is
mentioned by Mercutio in *Romeo and Juliet* (I, iv, 74):

> O'er ladies' lips, who straight on kisses dream,
> Which oft the angry Mab with blisters plagues ...

Two other feminine problems are very briefly and dis-
creetly touched upon. The Duchess of York refers to her
menopause and the end of child-bearing as her 'teeming
date', when she asks her husband (*King Richard II,* V, ii, 90):

> Have we more sons? or are we like to have?
> Is not my teeming date drunk up with time?

There is a very unusual and brief reference to menstruation:

> *Gonzalo.* ... as leaky as an unstanched wench.
> *The Tempest,* I, i, 45

Systemic disorders producing skin manifestations are a
common condition, and are possibly implied by the following, although a psychiatrist may read more into it (1 *King
Henry IV,* III, i, 27):

> Diseased nature oftentimes breaks forth
> In strange eruptions ...

A severe headache is described in a dialogue between

Othello and his wife, with a strong note of sympathy included (*Othello*, III, iii, 287):

> *Desdemona.*   Why do you speak so faintly?
> Are you not well?
> *Othello.* I have a pain upon my forehead here.
> *Desdemona.* ... Let me but bind it hard, within this hour
> It will be well.

Shakespeare's description of a dreadful headache, possibly migraine, is so succinct that one wonders whether he had suffered an attack. Not surprisingly, Juliet's poor nurse had one before her mistress' wedding! (*Romeo and Juliet*, II, v, 48):

> Lord, how my head aches! What a head have I!
> It beats as it would fall in twenty pieces.

Paracelsus (1493-1541), a medical revolutionary, who
opposed the long-standing reliance on the works
of Galen, and emphasised the value of observation
and experience. This portrait is from his *Erster
(-zehender) Theil der Bücher und Schrifften* (Basle,
1589 and 1590). (From *A Catalogue of Sixteenth
Century Medical Books in Edinburgh Libraries* compiled
by D. T. Bird, 1982; reproduced by courtesy
of the Royal College of Physicians of Edinburgh.)

17
THERAPEUTICS

Helena: Our remedies oft in ourselves do lie ...
All's Well that Ends Well, I, i, 202

N THE ELIZABETHAN AGE, which spanned the fifteenth and sixteenth centuries, the art and skills of therapeutics were modelled on principles which had been practised for several preceding centuries. The underlying theories were the doctrines of the four humours, which, together with the concept of 'natural', 'animal' and 'vital' spirits, afforded an explanation for the symptoms of most diseases. The basic properties of these four humours – namely, heat, cold, moisture and dryness – were considered of great importance to the human body, and constituted the rationale of therapeutics by diet, drugs, herbals and various physical means. According to the doctrine of contraries, heat would expel cold, and moisture would counteract dryness, so it was necessary to assess the quality and amount of each in the body, and then to administer some sort of treatment which was aimed at normalising the excess.

Medical methods were directed at the elimination of disease-producing humoral fluids. This was accomplished by purges (or 'clysters'), often of a rather severe type, or surgically by bleeding, leeching and cupping. All these were often used in turn, or even in combination. In addition, there were other auxiliary aids such as 'natural magic', in the form of charms, rings, amulets and so on. A legacy of this is the copper bracelet, still widely used for the 'treatment' of rheumatism and arthritis. Religious medals were sold at places of pilgrimage connected with common diseases, and were worn around the neck to ward off illnesses. These are still considered useful by many.

There can be no doubt that treatment by suggestion must have played a large part then as it does now. Timon, mentally ill himself, receives harsh treatment from his friends. He then advises the senators who try to appease him (V, i, 196) to:

> ... ease them of their griefs,
> Their fears of hostile strokes, their aches, losses,
> Their pangs of love, with other incident¹ throes
> That nature's fragile vessel doth sustain
> In life's uncertain voyage ...

In the same vein, Helicanus, one of the lords of Tyre, tells a depressed companion whose illness originated from the loss of a daughter and a wife (*Pericles*, V, i, 52):

> Sure, all's effectless; yet nothing we'll omit
> That bears recovery's name.

Treatment which acted through the mind was among the earliest employed by man. Even in the presence of the most desperate situations, good advice and reassurance will be of help in the worst cases. The ailing King Henry IV makes this same observation when, in desperation, he summons his knights in the early hours of the morning(2 *King Henry IV,* III, i, 39):

The preparation of medicines, from *The Practise of the New and Old Phisicke,* by K. Gesner, 1599. (From *A Catalogue of Sixteenth Century Medical Books in Edinburgh Libraries* compiled by D. T. Bird, 1982; reproduced by courtesy of the Royal College of Physicians of Edinburgh.)

King. How foul it is; what rank diseases grow,
And with what danger, near the heart of it.
Warwick. It is but as a body yet distempered;[2]
Which to his former strength may be restored
With good advice and little medicine.

A belief, which still exists, that divine intervention can work in some cases must have placed the priest-physician at an advantage, as he could profitably exploit the situation with the promise of divine healing. King Lear's daughter, Cordelia, expresses this belief when she implores her physician (IV, vii, 15):

O you kind gods,
Cure this great breach in his abused nature!

Likewise, Lady Macbeth's physician, unable to cure her obsessions and 'infected mind', gives away her case and admits (V, i, 72): 'More needs she the divine than the physician.'

Polypharmacy in large doses was the rule. Prescriptions were always written in Latin, for as Laurence Joubert, Dean of the Faculty of Medicine at Montpellier, correctly assumed: 'If prescriptions are published in the simple tongue the mob will take them and trade in them.' Latin has given way to the allegedly indecipherable scrawl that doctors are now supposed to write. Sophisticated physicians would prescribe 'cure-alls' with a proud boast that they had been in use for hundreds of years. Indeed, some were omitted from the British Pharmacopoeia only in 1786 at the insistence of Dr Heberden,* whilst others have continued to find a place in other official pharmacopoeias until quite recent times. The chief categories of medicinal preparations used at this

---

*William Heberden (1710-1801), well known for having described the rheumatic nodules on the phalanges called Heberden's nodes, was the first to describe angina pectoris in 1768. He also described chicken pox and night blindness, and in his *Commentarii de morborum historia et curatione*, which was published posthumously in 1802, he corrected some of the superstitious fallacies of polypharmacy.

time were syrups, juleps, decoctions, oils, linctuses, ointment, plaisters, troches, pills and poultices.

There are several references to poultices. Romeo explains to Benvolio the need for a poultice for treating their sword-fencing injuries (*Romeo and Juliet,* I, ii, 51):

> *Romeo.* Your plantain leaf is excellent for that.
> *Benvolio.* For what, I pray thee?
> *Romeo.* For your broken[3] shin.

And also (*Love's Labour's Lost,* III, i, 67):

> *Costard.* No enigma, no riddle, no l'envoy; no salve in the mail, sir. O, sir, plantain, a plain plantain; no l'envoy, no l'envoy; no salve, sir, but a plantain!

The plantain leaf, which was used as a poultice in the fore-going two references, was a broad-leafed weed growing in grass. It was a popular remedy for treating wounds and stings.

Juliet's nurse has problems with her arthritis – 'aching bones' – and suggests the remedy (*Romeo and Juliet,* II, v, 63): 'Is this the poultice for my aching bones?' Gloucester's eyes are gouged out on the orders of King Lear's brutal daughter, Goneril, and a faithful servant, who was ordered to thrust him out of his own house, provides relief (*King Lear,* III, vii, 105):

> ...I'll fetch some flax and whites of eggs
> To apply to his bleeding face.

The fiery Hotspur says (1 *King Henry IV,* I, iii, 57):

> ...the sovereignest[4] thing on earth
> Was parmaceti[3] for an inward bruise ...

The introduction of 'chemical remedies' by Paracelsus*
was an important advance. This was mainly aided by the failure of Galenical remedies and the humoral mechanism to
quell the ravages of syphilis, which was endemic in Europe.
Mercury had been used externally in the form of ointments
and fumigation for many years, and Paracelsus popularised
its use. Popular belief even imparted therapeutic value to
gold, a mineral which has a history as long as civilized man
himself. Prince Hal makes this observation when he is seen
trying on the crown of his dying father, King Henry, and defends himself (2 *King Henry IV*, IV, v, 161):

> Therefore thou best of gold art worst of gold,
> Other, less fine in carat, is more precious,
> Preserving life in med'cine potable[6]...

Cleopatra compares the very sight of her beloved Antony to
the beneficial effects of a dose of tincture of gold (I, v, 36):

> Yet, coming from him, that great med'cine hath
> With his tinct gilded thee.

Opium, although it is not so stated, or some other hypnotic concoction, is probably the drug alluded to in the following quotations:

> *Archidamus.* .... We will give you sleepy drinks, that your

---

*Paracelsus (1493-1541), whose real name was Philippus Aureolus Theophrastus
Bombastus Paracelsus von Hohenheim, ridiculed the four humours of Galen, and
even burnt his books in the market-place of Basle. However, like his contemporaries, his medicine was infused with the supernatural and the occult. He was
considered the 'eccentric father of chemistry and the reformer of materia medica',
and introduced many mineral substances, such as mercury, iron and arsenic into
medicine, as well as various tinctures, and laudanum.

senses, unintelligent of our insufficience,[7] may, though they cannot praise us, as little accuse us.

The Winter's Tale, I, i, 14

Lady Macbeth. . . . I have drugged their possets,[8]
That death and nature do contend about them,
Whether they live or die.

Macbeth, II, ii, 6

This probably applies also to the drug which Pisanio gave Imogen in the wilderness near Milford-Haven (*Cymbeline*, III, iv, 186):

Pisanio. . . . My noble mistress,
Here is a box; I had it from the Queen.
What's in't is precious. If you are sick at sea
Or stomach-qualm'd[9] at land, a dram of this
Will drive away distemper.

Pisanio gave it to her for sea-sickness or a queasy stomach, but it must have been strong stuff, for when Imogen later took it, it put her into a death-like sleep, from which she wakened to see the headless trunk of the despised Cloten in the clothes of her beloved Posthumus!

In addition to the usual herbal remedies and various mineral substances, many ingredients of animal origin, some quite repulsive, were also employed in treatment. Wine was frequently used as a vehicle for medicinal preparations or to extract the active properties of certain drugs. Until pharmacology was able to provide more effective results, drugs of all kinds were used and valued according to whether they were rare, expensive, and even unpleasant to smell or taste. Medicine has traditionally been considered to be bitter, and among the few references to bitter medicine, Proteus, one of

the two gentlement of Verona tells Valentine, the other gentleman (II, iv, 145):

> When I was sick you gave me bitter pills,
> And I must minister the like to you.

Isabella, revealing her plans to her companion, Mariana, says
(*Measure for Measure*, IV, vi, 7):

> I should not think it strange; for 'tis a physic
> That's bitter to sweet end.

Blood-letting was a standard therapeutic procedure and
had been utilised from the earliest times. The procedure was
intended to neutralise the humours; if they were interlocked
in abnormal proportions, then by drawing one off, the
natural ratio would be established. The quantity to be bled
depended upon the particular humour which was considered
to be predominant. Unfortunately, for very many years,
blood-letting or phlebotomy was practised to excess, and
much blood was spilt by over-zealous medical attendants
with no benefit whatsoever to their patients. The skin was
usually carefully prepared by warming, rubbing and massag-
ing, and a tourniquet was applied to compress the limb. The
blood was collected in a metal bowl in order to measure the
amount drawn off, and some estimation was made of the
time it took for the blood to separate.

Antony, viewing the bleeding corpse of Julius Caesar,
wonders (*Julius Caesar*, III, i, 153): 'Who else must be let
blood, who else is rank.' 'Rankness' was a medical state
usually requiring blood-letting; Oliver used this term when
he considered settling scores with his brother (*As You Like It,*
I, i, 78): 'I will physic your rankness.'

Vannesection amidst luxurious surrounds; an etching by Abraham
Bosse (1635). (Courtesy of Bibliothèque Nationale, Paris.)

The Archbishop of York, a leading rebel against King
Henry IV, resorts to the same allusion when he realises that
his forces are no match for the King's (2 *King Henry IV,* IV, i,
64):

> To diet rank minds sick of happiness,
> And purge th' obstructions which begin to stop
> Our very veins of life.

A purgative is still considered by many as a useful therapeutic measure, and perhaps it is. Macbeth (V, iii, 55) tells his doctor what he would like done to the English forces:

What rhubarb, senna or what purgative drug,
Would scour these English hence?

The enema or 'clyster' was another therapeutic weapon, and an alternative to the powerful effect of the usual mediaeval purgatives. Pliny,* writing on medical remedies which had been borrowed from animals, stated: 'A bird called the ibis makes use of Nile water and the curve of its beak to purge itself through the part by which it is most conducive to health for the residue of heavy foodstuffs to be excreted.' In this way the enema probably originated. It has come a long way from the apparatus of those days, which consisted of a dried pig's bladder into which a tube was fixed. This was greased and inserted into the patient's anus and the contents were expelled into the rectum. Ambroise Paré, the famous French surgeon, said of enemas: 'Doctors consider it to be beneath their dignity to sully their hands, and leave the administration of enemas to surgeons and apothecaries.' Iago, one of Othello's officers, noticed Cassio's attention to

---

*Pliny (A.D. 23-79), or Gaius Plinius Secundus, was born in Novum Comum (now Como) in Northern Italy. He was the author of many historical and technical works, including a 37 volume 'Natural History' which continued to be a reference work into the Middle Ages. He died trying to help refugees during the eruption of Mount Vesuvius.

Othello's wife, Desdemona, and planned intrigue between them (II, i, 177):

Yet again your fingers to your lips? Would they were clyster-pipes for your sake!

Aqua vitae, the water of life or ardent spirits, especially from the first distillation in a chemical process, was usually favoured by older women. It had a similar therapeutic value to our present-day smelling salts. There was much need for this in the tragic sequences of *Romeo and Juliet,* for the poor old nurse took all her lady's sorrows to heart (III, ii, 80):

Give me some aqua vitae.
These griefs, these woes, these sorrows, make me old.

And again (IV, v, 14):

Alas, alas! Help, help! my lady's dead!
O well-a-day that ever I was born!
Some aqua vitae, ho!

In the dialogue between Sir Toby Belch and a servant, the following reference to *aqua vitae* occurs (*Twelfth Night,* II, v, 173):

Sir Toby. Why, thou hast put him in such a dream that when the image of it leaves him he must run mad.
Maria. Nay, but say true; does it work upon him?
Sir Toby. Like aqua vitae with a midwife.

Elizabethan London was noted for its smells, lack of sanitation and poor hygiene. This situation had been accepted by a population of about 150 000 living in London in the early 1600s. Ross, a Scottish nobleman, gives an

account of the state of the country, describing the lament-
able conditions which would appear to have existed in London at that time (*Macbeth*, IV, iii, 165):

> Alas poor country,
> Almost afraid to know itself! It cannot
> Be call'd our mother, but our grave; where nothing,
> But who knows nothing, is once seen to smile;
> Where sighs, and groans, and shrieks, that rent the air,
> Are made, not mark'd; where violent sorrow seems
> A modern ecstacy; the dead man's knell
> Is there scarce ask'd for who; and good men's lives
> Expire before the flowers in their caps,
> Dying or ere they sicken.

Elaborate instructions were issued by civil authorities to
keep the streets clean and hopefully to reduce infection,
especially at threats of approaching plague. In 1547 all wells
and pumps in plague-infected areas were drawn three times
a week, and at each drawing twelve bucketfuls of water were
poured into 'channels' which ran along the middle of many
streets. Naturally, these channels became gutters which harboured filth instead of carrying it away. Mistress Quickly, a
prostitute, has her anger aroused (2 *King Henry IV*, II, i, 44)
when Falstaff says of her: 'Throw the quean in the channel.'
There could be no worse place for a person to land! No
wonder, therefore, that the gentry, the wealthy and those who
could afford it were advised to move to a better climate.

> *Gaunt.* Devouring pestilence[10] hangs in our air
> And thou art flying to a fresher clime.
> > *King Richard, II*, I, iii, 284

The dangers of a bad atmosphere are also mentioned in these lines:

> *Leontes.*   The blessed gods
> Purge all infections from our air whilst you
> Do climate here!
>> *The Winter's Tale,* V, i, 168

> *Brutus.* It is not for your health thus to commit
> Your weak condition to the raw cold morning.
>> *Julius Caesar,* II, i, 235

The humours, the cause of most illnesses, were influenced by the climate as a 'corruption of the air':

> So it is, beseiged with sable-coloured[11] melancholy, I did commend the black oppressing humour[12] to the most wholesome physic of thy health-giving air ..
>> *Love's Labour's Lost,* I, i, 225

In the environment of those dark ages, quacks and their cures abounded. If a patient entrusted himself to one of them, well, it was his own fault, as the sickly old John of Gaunt relates (*King Richard II,* II, i, 97):

> And thou, too careless patient as thou art,
> Commit'st thy anointed body to the cure
> Of those physicians that first wounded thee ...

Among other references to quackery are the following:

> *King.*   I say we must not
> So stain our judgement, or corrupt our hope,
> To prostitute our past-cure malady
> To empirics;[13] or to dissever so
> Our great self and our credit to esteem
> A senseless help, when help past sense we deem.
>> *All's Well that Ends Well,* II, i, 118

[251]

Doctor. There are a crew of wretched souls
That stay his cure.[14] Their malady convinces
The great assay of art;[15] but at his touch,
Such sanctity hath heaven given his hand,
They presently[16] amend.

Macbeth, IV, iii, 141

In the foregoing lines from Macbeth is a reference to the divine power of kings to cure by 'touching'. Tuberculous involvement of the lymph glands, formerly called scrofula, was a common disease in those days, and is common even now in some countries. The disease was also called 'the King's evil', because many people believed that a victim could be healed if the King 'touched' him. The practice is supposed to have originated with the Anglo-Saxon king, Edward the Confessor, in the tenth century, and to have been continued by all succeeding monarchs until William III, who was reported to have discontinued it. The laying on of hands and faith healing, in one form or another, has persisted even to this day. Malcolm gives a description of 'touching' for the King's Evil in *Macbeth* (IV, iii, 146):

'Tis called the evil:
A most miraculous work in this good king;
Which often since my here-remain in England
I have seen him do. How he solicits heaven,
Himself best knows; but strangely-visited people,
All swoln and ulcerous,[17] pitiful to the eye,
The mere despair of surgery, he cures,
Hanging a golden stamp about their necks,
Put on with holy prayers; and 'tis spoken,
To the succeeding royalty he leaves
The healing benediction.

[252]

This engraving from a 1556 manuscript shows Queen
Mary 'touching' a subject for the King's Evil
(tuberculous glands). In the Middle Ages mysticism
and symbolic procedures were prevalent, and the Royal
Touch was thought to be of therapeutic importance.

Shakespeare briefly touched on the obvious therapeutic
value of rest (*King Lear,* IV, iv, 12):

Doctor. Our foster-nurse of nature is repose ...

And (*Winter's Tale,* II, iii, 10):

Servant.   He took good rest tonight;
'Tis hop'd his sickness is discharg'd.[18]

'The Royal Touch'. The French King Henry IV 'touching' scrofulous patients to 'cure' them. The Kings of France inherited this power from their relatives the Kings of England. Frontispiece of *De mirabili Strumas sanandi vi*, 1609. (From *A History of Medicine* by A. Castiglioni, 1941.)

He also made an appropriate reference to the value of good medicine and good medical treatment in general; Rosalind tells her Orlando (*As You Like It*, III, ii, 333): 'I will not cast away my physic but on those that are sick.' Jaques, attending on his banished Duke, tells him (*As You Like It*, II, vii, 60) that he will:

Cleanse the foul body of th' infected world,
If they will patiently receive my medicine.

[254]

And in another play, Cornelius the physician says (*Cymbeline*, V, v, 255):

> A certain stuff, which, being ta'en, would cease[19]
> The present pow'r of life, but in short time
> All offices of nature should again
> Do their due functions.

After Othello's epileptic fit, Iago remarks (IV, i, 44): 'Work on, my medicine, work!'

The medical doctrine of crisis has been universally prevalent, and the following passage refers to this (*King John*, III, iv, 112):

> *Pandulph*. Before the curing of a strong disease,
> Even in the instant of repair and health,
> The fit is strongest; evils that take leave
> On their departure most of all show evil ...

Nowadays, losing weight, jogging and exercising are an essential part of medical therapeutics. The gouty Falstaff, repenting and concerned about his obesity and advancing years, says (1 *King Henry IV*, V, iv, 163):

> If I do grow great, I'll grow less; for I'll purge, and leave sack, and live cleanly, as a nobleman should do.

On the healthful value of jogging, Autolycus, a wandering pedlar, sings (*Winter's Tale*, IV, iii, 118):

> Jog on, jog on, the footpath way,
>   And merrily hent[20] the stile-a;
> A merry heart goes all the day,
>   Your sad tires in a mile-a.

Which only goes to show how much ahead of his time Shakespeare was.

A proper diagnosis precedes all treatment, and this point is made when Hamlet's stepfather and mother, the King and Queen of Denmark, discuss his melancholic illness (II, ii, 54):

He tells me ... he hath found
The head and source of all your son's distemper.

And (II, ii, 100):

Polonius.   and now remains
That we find out the cause of this effect;
Or rather say the cause of this defect,
For this effect defective comes by cause.

A good physician never leaves a patient without imparting some atmosphere of hope. The same good intention is expressed in *Antony and Cleopatra* (II, v, 85):

Though it be honest, it is never good
To bring bad news.

And in *Measure for Measure* (III, i, 2):

The miserable have no other medicine
But only hope:

The taking of a good history is an essential part of good medicine, and is referred to as follows (2 *King Henry IV,* III, i, 80):

Warwick. There is a history in all men's lives,
Figuring the natures of the times deceas'd;
The which observ'd a man may prophesy,
With a near aim, of the main chance of things
As yet not come to life ...

Too many consultations or 'sittings' can be tedious, as many patients will readily point out, echoing the words of Lord Say (2 *King Henry VI*, IV, vii, 82):

> Long sitting to determine poor men's causes
> Hath made me full of sickness and diseases.

A controlled clinical trial is an important method by which a new drug can find its place in therapeutics. Apart from volunteers, prisoners have been used for clinical trials in many centres; this method of experimentation was first suggested by Antonio Brasalova in 1534. He was a physician to Pope Paul III, and advocated the testing of drugs which possessed doubtful clinical properties on condemned criminals. It may have been this which prompted the Queen in *Cymbeline* to inform her doctor that the poison he was to supply her with should be tried on prisoners destined for hanging (I, v, 18):

> I will try the forces
> Of these thy compounds on such creatures as
> We count not worth the hanging – but none human –
> To try the vigour of them, and apply
> Allayments to their act, and by them gather
> Their several virtues and effects.

Finally, after treatment comes convalescence and support, and this is briefly suggested by Timon, a sickly character himself (I, i, 110):

> 'Tis not enough to keep the feeble up,
> But to support him after.

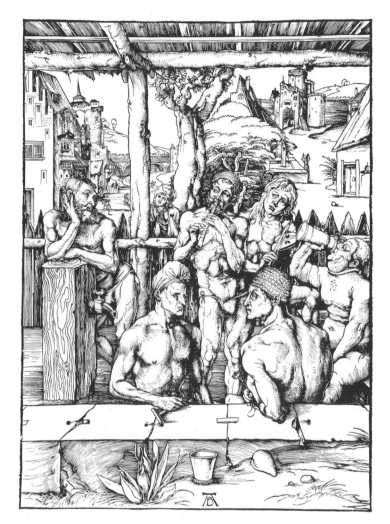

'Men's Bath', woodcut by Albrecht Dürer (1471-1528).
Reproduced from *Medicine and the Artist (Ars Medica)*
by permission of the Philadelphia Museum of
Art; Dover Publications, Inc., New York.

18
SEX IN
SHAKESPEARE

T WOULD PROBABLY surprise most people to know that Shakespeare's references to sex are numerous. He made very many references to sexual activity, sexual encounters, prostitutes, the male and female sexual organs, and various other related topics. However, like a true gentleman, his references and words were never crude or explicit, but were clouded in elaborate imagery, deliberate ambiguity and double meaning. The word 'prostitute', for example, is seldom used as a noun, but instead we read of a 'strumpet', 'wanton', 'courtesan', 'guinea-hen', 'beagle', 'callet', 'heifer', 'hobby-horse' – to mention just a few synonyms. One of his famous brothel keepers, Mistress Overdone, was referred to as a 'bawd', and whereas a frequenter of brothels was a 'fleshmonger' or 'whoremaster', a womaniser was a 'chamberer' or a 'bed-presser'! Very few of these terms are coarse, but their deliberate ambivalence is a marked feature of Shakespeare's sexual descriptions. When he talks of the sexual act, we read of such polite but unusual terms as 'foining', 'execution', 'groping', 'horsemanship', 'pricking' and so on. The sexual organs also have their share of unusual descriptions, again more often than not associated with double

meaning. The female 'lap' has a sexual connotation, and one of its double meanings is intended to represent a woman's genital area. From this we go on to read of 'Pillicock Hill', 'secret things', 'maidenhead', 'chaste treasure', 'Venus' glove' and so on, while the female breasts are 'cliffs', 'mamonets', 'fountains'. 'Thing' is both female and male, and more descriptive terms for the male genital organ include 'pike', 'dribbling dart of love', 'lance', 'prick', 'tail', 'instrument', 'three-inch fool', 'tool', and other miscellaneous synonyms.

Shakespeare's views on love and sex are expressed with a remarkable degree of pertinence. He does not go into technical details, but by diversifying his terms, punning and using words of double and even triple meaning, he has provided many unique sexual descriptions. Take for example the famous lines from one of his long poems, *Venus and Adonis*. Venus, the goddess of love, is sexually roused and while embracing Adonis tries to convert his unwillingness to desire and love making.* The double meaning of many words is very typical, and the general meaning of the passage is obvious:

> 'Fondling'[1] she saith, 'since I have hemm'd thee here
> Within the circuit of this ivory pale,[2]
> I'll be a park, and thou shalt be my deer;

---

*Venus, the goddess of love and beauty in Greek mythology, loved two mortals, one of whom was Adonis. He was killed while hunting a wild boar, and Venus in her grief changed his blood into a flower which is called the anemone or windflower. Proserpina restored him to life, but he had to spend six months of the year with her in the lower world; the other six months he could spend with Venus. This myth helped to explain the rebirth of nature in spring.

Feed where thou wilt, on mountain or in dale;
Graze on my lips, and if those hills be dry,
Stray lower, where the pleasant fountains lie.
'Within this limit is relief enough,
Sweet bottom-grass³ and high delightful plain,
Round rising hillocks, brakes⁴ obscure and rough,
To shelter thee from tempest and from rain;
Then be my deer, since I am such a park;
No dogs shall rouse thee,⁵ though a thousand bark.'

Venus and Adonis, 229-240

Falstaff, a favourite in many plays, is noted for his vulgarity, his gluttony, and his frequenting of brothels and keeping company with loose ladies. He tells Doll Tearsheet, a prostitute, one of the regulars at the Boar's Head Tavern:

Falstaff. For to serve bravely is to come halting off; you know, to come off the breach with his *pike*⁶ bent bravely, and to surgery bravely; to venture upon the *charg'd chambers* bravely –
Doll. Hang yourself, you muddy conger,⁷ hang yourself!

2 King Henry IV, II, iv, 49

The word 'breach' ('breach with his pike') is an example of the double meaning which occurs in many sexual descriptions and is supposed to refer to the vulval area. The word 'breach' is also used in *All's Well that Ends Well* – again, with double meaning – in the dialogue between Helena and Parolles on

N.B. The italics in the quotations in this chapter are those of the author.

another sexual topic, this time virginity (I, i, 114):

> *Helena.* Bless our poor virginity from underminers and blowers-up! Is there no military policy how virgins might blow up men?
> *Parolles.* Virginity being blown down,[8] man will quicklier be blown up; marry,[9] in blowing him down again, with the *breach* yourselves made, you lose your city. It is not politic in the commonwealth of nature to preserve virginity. Loss of virginity is rational[10] increase; and there was never virgin got[11] till virginity was first lost. That you were made of is metal[12] to make virgins. Virginity by being once lost may be ten times found; by being ever kept, it is ever lost. 'Tis too cold a companion; away with 't.

Among the many different references to the female genitals, Shakespeare used the word 'lap' several times. When its sexual connotations are read between the lines, the following apparently innocent passage from *Hamlet* becomes interesting (III, ii, 108):

> *Hamlet.* Lady, shall I *lie in your lap?*
> *Ophelia.* No, my lord.
> *Hamlet.* I mean, my head upon your lap?
> *Ophelia.* Ay, my lord.
> *Hamlet.* Do you think I meant country matters?[13]
> *Ophelia.* I think nothing, my lord.
> *Hamlet.* That's a fair thought to *lie between maids' legs.*

The Duke of Suffolk, in 2 *King Henry VI*, was the Queen's lover. He was conveniently banished by the King, but got together with the Queen for a few moments and gave vent to his suppressed feelings (III, ii, 388):

> *Suffolk.* If I depart from thee I cannot live;

And in thy sight to die, what were it else
But like a pleasant slumber *in thy lap?*
Here could I breathe my soul into the air,
As mild and gentle as the cradle-babe
Dying with mother's dug[14] between its lips;
Where, from thy sight, I should be raging mad
And cry out for thee to close up mine eyes,
To have thee with thy lips to stop my mouth; ...

Hotspur, about to charge off to a battle, tries to coax a last embrace from his wife 1 *King Henry IV,* III, i, 228):

Hotspur. Come, Kate, *thou art perfect in lying down.*
Come, quick, quick, that I may lay my head *in thy lap.*
Lady Percy. Go, ye giddy goose.

The female thighs, as well as the parts between them, are referred to by Mercutio, a friend of Romeo, using the unusual word 'demesnes' in the same sense as 'lap' is used in the previous passages (*Romeo and Juliet,* II, i, 19):

By her fine foot, straight leg, and quivering thigh,
And the *demesnes* that there adjacent lie ...

Another passage from *Hamlet* (II, ii, 227) speaks of the same location; again, the double meaning is eloquently phrased:

Guildenstern. Happy in that we are not over-happy;
On fortune's cap we are not the very button.[15]
Hamlet. Nor the soles of her shoe?
Rosencrantz. Neither, my lord.
Hamlet. Then you live *about her waist,* or in the *middle of her favours?*
Guildenstern. Faith, her *privates* we.

[263]

Hamlet. In the secret parts of Fortune? O, most true, she is a strumpet.

A discreet pun is used on the word 'privates' or private parts; whereas Guildenstern means that he and Rosencrantz are merely 'private' soldiers in Fortune's service, he is also referring to the 'private parts' of the body.

Mistress Quickly, talking to Falstaff, misuses the word 'erection' when referring to another prostitute, Mistress Ford. Shakespeare intended that prostitutes should be ignorant, and should speak with rough usage of the English language (*Merry Wives of Windsor*, III, v, 34):

Mistress Quickly. She does so take on with her men; they mistook their *erection.*

In the following quotation, erection is intended to mean 'direction', when Timon instructs a couple of prostitutes (*Timon of Athens,* IV, iii, 161):

Plague all,
That your activity may defeat and quell
The *source of all erection.*

The sexual act is frequently described, usually as a dialogue, which is often frank and witty. Bertram, Count of Rousillon, was a remarkable young man who, according to Samuel Johnson's judgement: 'married Helen as a coward, leaves her as a profligate; when she is dead by his unkindness, sneaks home to a second marriage, is accused by a woman whom he has wronged, defends himself by falsehood, and is dismissed by happiness!' If this is so, his boasts come as no surprise! (*All's Well That Ends Well,* V, iii, 208):

> Certain it is I lik'd her,
> And *boarded* her i' the wanton way of youth.

Not surprisingly, Romeo and Juliet provide a fair number of examples of Shakespearean allusions to sex. In the opening lines of this play we read (I, i, 22):

Sampson. . . . I will be civil with the maids – I will cut off their heads.
Gregory. The heads of the maids?
Sampson. Ay, the heads of the maids, or their *maidenheads;* take it in what sense thou wilt.

. . .

Gregory. . . . *Draw thy tool;* here comes two of the house of Montagues.
Sampson. My *naked weapon is out.*

Further on in *Romeo and Juliet* (II, iv, 85):

Mercutio. Why, is not this better now than groaning for love? . . . for this drivelling love is like a great natural that runs lolling up and down to *hide his bauble*[16] *in a hole.*
Benvolio. Stop there, stop there.
Mercutio. Thou desirest me to stop in my *tale*[17] *against the hair.*
Benvolio. Thou wouldst else have made *thy tale large.*
Mercutio. O, thou art deceiv'd: I would have made it short; for I was come to the whole depth of my tale . . .

. . .

Nurse. Is it good den?
Mercutio. 'Tis no less, I tell ye; for the bawdy hand of the *dial* is now upon the *prick* of noon.
Nurse. Out upon you! What a man are you?

The 'dial', a clock's dial, is twice used as a metaphor to refer to the female genitalia. In addition to Mercutio's remark above, Prince Hal speaks to Falstaff (1 *King Henry IV,* I, ii, 9): ' ... *dials* the signs of *leaping-houses.*' A 'leaping house' is, in this case, a brothel!

Another example of deliberate ambiguity occurs with the word 'medlar'. The medlar tree produced a fruit like a brown apple, which was eaten only when it had matured and softened. In *Romeo and Juliet,* the word is used with a quibble on 'medlar', a term used frequently by Shakespeare to refer to the genital area (II, i, 33):

> If love be blind, love cannot hit the mark.
> Now will he sit under a *medlar tree,*
> And wish his mistress were that kind of fruit
> As maids call *medlars* when they laugh alone.

In *As You Like It* (III, ii, 106):

> *Touchstone.* Truly, the tree yields bad fruit.
> *Rosalind.* I'll graff[18] it with you, and then I shall graff it with a *medlar.* Then it will be the earliest fruit i' th' country; for you'll be rotten ere you be half ripe, and that's the right virtue of the *medlar.*

The longest dialogue containing many sexual innuendoes occurs in *Much Ado About Nothing.* It takes place in the apartment of a lady called Hero. The conversation is between the lady and Margaret, her servant (III, iv, 22):

> *Hero.* God give me joy to wear it, for my heart is exceeding heavy.
> *Margaret.* 'Twill be heavier soon, *by the weight of a man.*

The next fifty lines of this passage are a bawdy dialogue between the two women.

Elizabethan plays abound in references to 'cuckolds' and 'horns', and Shakespeare's were no exception. He used the word 'cuckold' and its related terms 'cuckold-mad', 'cuckold-maker' and 'cuckoldy' very frequently. A cuckold was a husband whose wife had deceived him, and who was therefore considered a joke by his friends. The name is derived from the cuckoo, a bird which does not build its own nest, but instead lays its eggs in the nest of another, usually smaller bird, who innocently hatches and feeds the foster-fledgling cuckoo. The original meaning of the word 'cuckold' may thus be 'one who has been cheated by a cuckoo'. To 'cry cuckoo' after a man was to warn him that his wife's lover was nearby:

> The cuckoo then on every tree
> Mocks married men, for this sings he:
> 'Cuckoo;
> Cuckoo, cuckoo' – O word of fear,
> Unpleasing to a married ear!
>
> *Love's Labour's Lost,* V, ii, 885

A cuckold was also supposed to wear a pair of invisible horns as the sign of an unhappy fate. The origin of this curious myth is unknown, though there have been a few theories. One is that horns arose from the legend of an amorous god, Jupiter, who was self-transformed into the likeness of a bull.* Possibly horns were appropriate for a

---

* '... the goodly transformation of Jupiter there, his brother, the bull, the primitive statue and oblique memorial of cuckolds, a thrifty shoeing-horn in a chain ...' (*Troilus and Cressida,* V, i, 45)

[267]

cuckold because he had shown himself a stupid, ox-like crea-
ture. Once the connection between horns and infidelity had
been established, then endless play was made on the word
'horn' in all its possible uses and sexual meanings – for instance, 'he would have been horn-mad' (*Merry Wives of Windsor,* I, iv, 43), that is, mad as a stag in spring, or more simply,
very angry at having been cuckolded. An example of this
horn-madness is represented in this dialogue (*Comedy of
Errors,* II, i, 56):

> *Adriana.* It seems he hath great care to please his wife.
> *Dromio of Ephesus.* Why, mistress, sure my master is *horn-
> mad.*[19]
> *Adriana. Horn-mad,* thou villain!
> *Dromio.* I mean not *cuckold-mad;*
> But, sure, he is stark mad.

In the following passage (2 *King Henry IV,* I, ii, 41) Falstaff puns on the three meanings of horn: (i) the cuckold's
horn, supposed to be worn by every husband deceived by his
wife; (ii) the cornucopia or horn of abundance, the mytholo-
gical symbol of a horn overflowing with fruits; and (iii) the
horny sides of a lantern (horn being used before glass):

> Well, he may sleep in security;[20] for he hath the *horn* of abund-
> ance, and the lightness of his wife shines through it; and yet
> cannot he see ...

From *Much Ado About Nothing* (II, i, 19) comes another
joke on cuckold's horns, possibly meaning the penis, using a
common proverb of those days to the effect that a bad-
tempered cow has the least power to hurt with her horns:

> *Beatrice.* Too curst is more than curst. I shall lessen God's

sending that way; for, it is said 'God sends a curst cow *short horns;* but to a cow too curst he sends none.

Further on in the same play we read (II, i, 36):

Beatrice. No; but to the gate, and there will the devil meet me, like an old cuckold, with *horns* on his head, and say 'Get you to heaven, Beatrice, get you to heaven; here's no place for you maids'.

And again (V, ii, 33):

Benedick. ... I can find out no rhyme to 'lady' but 'baby' – an innoncent rhyme; for 'scorn', 'horn' – a *hard* rhyme; for 'school', 'fool' – a babbling rhyme; very ominous *endings.*

Also, in *All's Well that Ends Well* (II, ii, 23) we read:

Clown. ... as the nail to his *hole,* the cuckold to his *horn* ...

The horn is used to indicate the penis on other occasions, and rather rudely in the discussion between Lavinia, the daughter of Titus Andronicus, and the adulterous Tamora, Queen of the Goths (*Titus Andronicus,* II, iii, 61):

Tamora. Had I the pow'r that some say Dian had,
Thy temples should be planted presently[21]
With *horns,* as was Actaeon's,* and the hounds
Should drive upon thy new-transform'd limbs,
Unmannerly intruder as thou art!

---

*Actaeon gazed on the goddess Diana while she and her nymphs were bathing. As a punishment he was turned into a stag. His own hounds attacked him and tore him to pieces.

Lavinia. Under your patience, gentle Emperess
'Tis thought you have a *goodly gift in horning*,[22]
And to be doubted[23] that your Moor and you
Are singled[24] forth to *try experiments*.

The brothel scene in *Pericles* (IV, ii) is quite remarkable for its sexual overtones. The brothel-keeper has been moaning about the poor quality of his whores, and considers himself fortunate that a beautiful girl, Marina, has been sold to him by pirates. He sends the procurer of his establishment (Bawd) out on the street to proclaim her virtues:

Pander. We lost too much money in this mart[25] by being too wenchless.†
Bawd. We were never so much out of creatures. We have but poor three, and they can do no more than they can do; and they with *continual action are even as good as rotten.*
Pander. Therefore let's have fresh ones ...
Boult. ... But shall I search the market?
Bawd. What else, man? The stuff we have, a strong wind will blow it to pieces, they are so *pitifully sodden.*[26]
Pander. Thou sayest true; they are too unwholesome ...

Marina is now brought in; she has 'a good face, speaks well, and has excellent good clothes'. Pander tells the bawd to 'take her in, instruct her what she has to do, that she may not be raw in her entertainment'.[27] Bawd then gives further instructions:

Bawd. Boult, take you the marks of her – the colour of her hair, complexion, height, her age, with warrant of her virginity; and

---

† The pander's business was to bring in clients; the bawd (a woman) managed the brothel.

Boult (Patrick Wymark), Marina (Geraldine McEwan), and Bawd (Angela Baddeley), in Act IV, Scene II, of a production of *Pericles* by the Shakespeare Memorial Theatre in 1958. Photograph by Angus McBean: reproduced by courtesy of the Shakespeare Birthplace Trust.

cry, 'He that will give most shall have her first'. Such a *maiden-head* were no cheap thing, if men were as they have been.
Boult. Performance shall follow.

Marina is naturally not happy with her situation, being placed in a brothel!

[271]

Bawd. Ay, and you shall live in pleasure.
Marina. No.
Bawd. Yes, indeed shall you, and taste gentlemen of all fashions. You shall fare well; you shall have the difference of all complexions ...[28]

...

Marina. The gods defend me!
Bawd. If it please the gods to defend you by men, then men must comfort you, men must feed you, *men must stir you up.*

...

Boult. O, take her home, mistress, take her home. These blushes of hers must be quench'd with some present practice.

Marina, however, is not prepared to allow herself to be sacrificed easily:

Marina. If fires be hot, knives sharp, or waters deep,
Untied I still my virgin knot will keep.

Another famous brothel scene with Falstaff as the main character occurs in *2 Henry IV* (II, iv), and there are others. Many of the words for a prostitute are coarse, but unique. The word or phrase is designed to suit the scene, or the speaker, or the event. Usually it is a consonant of all these factors. Shakespeare used the word 'prostitute' (which is derived from the Latin *prostituere,* 'to put up for sale') infrequently, but never as a noun. For example, Marina says in her self-defence to the brothel keeper (*Pericles,* IV, vi, 187):

Prove that I cannot, take me home again
And *prostitute* me to the basest groom
That doth frequent your home.

Physicians visiting a patient suffering from plague,
apparently a rich man who could afford three
attendants. From Brunschwig's *Chirurgia* (1500).
(From *A History of Medicine* by A. Castiglioni, 1941.)

Surgery on the battlefield. Wars provided a good
training ground for barber-surgeons. The surgeon
here is Ambroise Paré, whose observations on
wounded soldiers led to the abandonment of
boiling oil as a treatment for gunshot wounds, and
to a reduction in sepsis and surgical trauma.
(Courtesy of the World Health Organization, Geneva.)

Instead he used far more descriptive terms to describe a prostitute, for example:

A beagle:

> *Timon.* Get thee away, and take
> Thy *beagles* with thee.
>
> Timon of Athens, IV, iii, 173

A callet:

> *Edward.* To make this shameless *callet* know herself.
>
> 3 King Henry VI, II, ii, 145

> *Emilia.* He call'd her whore. A beggar in his drink
> Could not have laid such terms upon his *callat.*
>
> Othello, IV, ii, 121

> *Leontes.*   A *callat*
> Of boundless tongue, who late hath beat her husband,
> And now baits me!
>
> The Winter's Tale, II, iii, 90

A common customer and commoner:

> *The King.* I think thee now some *common customer.*
>
> All's Well that Ends Well, V, iii, 280

> *Diana.* He gave it to a *commoner* o' th' camp ...
>
> All's Well that Ends Well, V, iii, 192

> *Othello.* O thou public *commoner!*
>
> Othello, IV, ii, 74

A drab:

> *Shepherd.* Dost thou deny thy father, cursed *drab?*
>
> 1 King Henry VI, V, iv, 32

Hamlet. Must, like a whore, unpack my heart with words,
And fall a-cursing, like a very *drab,*
A scullion!

Hamlet, II, ii, 581

A punk:

Lucio. ... she may be a *punk;* for many of them are neither
maid, widow, nor wife.

Measure for Measure, V, i, 179

Clown. ... your French crown for your taffety punk ...
All's Well that Ends Well, II, ii, 21

A strumpet:

York. Strumpet, thy words condemn thy brat and thee.
1 *King Henry VI,* V, iv, 84

Iago. ... 'tis the *strumpet's* plague
To beguile many and be beguil'd by one.

Othello, IV, i, 96

A trot:

Grumio. ... give him gold enough and marry him to ... an old
trot ... though she have as many diseases as two and fifty
horses.

Taming of the Shrew, I, ii, 76

We have seen how Shakespeare concealed his descriptions of sexual activity with deliberate ambiguity and words of double meaning. Consider another example, the three-way conversation between the Duke of Orleans, Louis the Dauphin, and the Constable of France (*King Henry V,* III, vii, 44):

Orleans. Your mistress *bears well.*

Dauphin. Me well; which is the prescript[29] praise and perfection of a good and particular mistress.
Constable. Nay, for methought yesterday your mistress shrewdly *shook your back.*
Dauphin. So perhaps did yours.
Constable. Mine was not *bridled.*
Dauphin. O, then belike she was old and gentle; and you *rode* like a kern of Ireland, your French hose off and in your straight strossers.[30]
Constable. You have good judgement in *horsemanship.*
Dauphin. Be warn'd by me, then: they that *ride* so, and *ride* not warily, fall into *foul bogs.* I had rather have my horse to my mistress.
Constable. I had as lief have my mistress a jade.[31]

King Lear abounds in animal images – 'hog in sloth, fox in stealth, wolf in greediness, dog in madness, lion in prey' – as if Shakespeare wished to portray a world in which many men and women are beasts, and only an exceptional few redeem

"Nature from the general curse." Lear provides a 'pell-mell' mixture of copulation images and epigrams (IV, vi, 110):

Adultery?
Thou shalt not die. Die for adultery? No.
The wren goes to't, and the small gilded fly
Does lecher[32] in my sight.
Let copulation thrive; for Gloucester's bastard son
Was kinder to his father than my daughters
Got 'tween the lawful sheets.
To't, luxury,[33] pell-mell, for I lack soldiers.
Behold yond simp'ring dame
Whose face *between her forks* presages snow,*

---

*A curious reference to the pubic hair, which whitens last on the human body.

That minces virtue[34] and does shake the head
To hear of pleasure's name –
The fitchew[35] nor the soiled horse[36] goes to't
With a more riotous appetite.
Down from the waist they are centaurs[37]
Though women all above;
But to the girdle do the gods inherit,
Beneath is all the fiends';
There's hell, there's darkness, there is the sulphurous pit –
Burning, scalding stench, consumption.

There are more references to prostitutes and venereal disease in *Timon of Athens* than in any other play. Timon is accosted in a cave by two prostitutes, who ask him for money. He is a noble Athenian, but swears at them in the language of their trade (IV, iii, 133):

Phrynia & Timandra. Give us some gold, good Timon.
Hast thou more?
Timon. Enough to make a whore forswear her trade,
And to make whores a bawd. Hold up, you sluts,
Your aprons mountant;[38] you are not oathable,
Although I know you'll swear, terribly swear,
Into strong shudders and to heavenly agues,
Th' immortal gods that hear you. Spare your oaths;
I'll trust to your conditions. Be whores still;
And he whose pious breath seeks to convert you –
Be strong in whore, allure him, burn him up;
Let your close fire predominate his smoke,[39]
And be no turncoats. Yet may your pains six months
Be quite contrary![40] And thatch your poor thin roofs
With burdens of the dead[41] – some that were hang'd,
No matter. Wear them, betray with them. Whore still;
Paint till a horse may mire upon your face.
A pox of wrinkles![42]

In a famous passage from *The Comedy of Errors* (III, ii, 107) Antipholus and Dromio discuss an exceedingly fat 'kitchen-wench' who is being considered as a bride for one of them. The comparison of various parts of this lady's anatomy with different countries, and the sexual inferences that can be read between the lines, are left to the reader's imagination:

Antipholus. What's her name?

Dromio. Nell, sir; . . .

Antipholus. Then she bears some breadth?

Dromio. No longer from head to foot than from hip to hip: she is spherical, like a globe; I could find out countries in her.

Antipholus. In what part of her body stands Ireland?

Dromio. Marry, sir, in her buttocks; I found it out by the bogs.

Antipholus. Where Scotland?

Dromio. I found it by the barrenness, hard in the palm of the hand.

Antipholus. Where France?

Dromio. In her forehead; arm'd and reverted, making war against her heir.

Antipholus. Where England?

Dromio. I look'd for the chalky cliffs, but I could find no whiteness in them; but I guess it stood in her chin, by the salt rheum[43] that ran between France and it.

Antipholus. Where Spain?

Dromio. Faith, I saw it not, but I felt it hot in her breath.

Antipholus. Where America, the Indies?

Dromio. O, sir, upon her nose, all o'er embellished with rubies, carbuncles,[44] sapphires, declining their rich aspect[45] to the hot breath of Spain; who sent whole armadoes of caracks[46] to the ballast[47] at her nose.

Antipholus. Where stood Belgia, the Netherlands?

Dromio. O, sir, I did not look so low.

Sir Henry Irving as Shylock in *The Merchant of
Venice* (Act I, Scene III), From *The Complete Works
of William Shakespeare* (c. 1910). Photograph:
Lydell Sawyer, London.

19
WOUNDS
&
SURGEONS

HE CRAFT of surgery was nourished throughout the Middle Ages by the turbulent state of nations, whose battles fostered the art of traumatic surgery. Most surgeons were trained in wars; Ambroise Paré (1510-1590), a great French surgeon, was a notable example. Unlike his colleagues, Paré was "unlettered", and, without the benefit of a formal education, was unhampered by the dogma and prejudice which affected other scholars of his time. He applied his keen brain and acute powers of observation to surgical practice, and thereby introduced many basic innovations such as the ligature and artery forceps, principles of sick nursing and after-care, treatment of fractures, good bandaging and splinting. Like his contemporaries, however, he believed in magical intervention, astrology and demons as a causative factor in disease. A translation of his surgical works became available in England in 1634, whereas the structure of the human body, as described by Andreas Vesalius (1514-1563), had appeared in London a century earlier, in 1545. Shakespeare's plays were written between 1588 and 1613, and in them we find many references to wounds and surgeons, which would re-

In this woodcut (c. 1560), King Henry II of France is shown on his deathbed, with Ambroise Paré and Andreas Vesalius in attendance. The King had named Paré a master surgeon on the sole grounds of his great ability, in spite of his lack of formal academic training. (National Library of Medicine, Bethesda.)

flect the current surgical knowledge of those days.

The barbers joined with the Guild of Surgeons as the United Company of Barber-Surgeons in 1540; this gave both barbers and surgeons professional recognition. Each was strictly forbidden to tamper with the craft of the other, except for tooth-drawing, which was common ground. The separation of the surgeons from the barbers must have been a contentious issue, because Shakespeare never mentioned the barbers in this context in his plays, and yet had many things to say about 'surgeons'. For instance, Theseus and Lysander are confronted with the body of Pyramus, who has stabbled himself, and realise the need for a surgeon (*Midsummer Night's Dream*, V, i, 300):

Lysander. Less than an ace, man; for he is dead; he is nothing.
Theseus. With the help of a surgeon he might yet recover and yet prove an ass.

When Shylock insists on his pound of flesh from Antonio, a Merchant of Venice, Portia is cautious as to the outcome (*Merchant of Venice*, IV, i, 252):

Have by some surgeon, Shylock, on your charge,
To stop his wounds, lest he do bleed to death.

Othello orders away Montano, his predecessor in the government of Cyprus, and one senses a tone of regret (II, iii, 245): 'Sir, for your hurts, myself will be your surgeon.'

Macbeth is a play full of horrors; a bleeding soldier is aided by Duncan, the Scottish King (I, ii, 43):

Sergeant. But I am faint; my gashes cry for help.
Duncan. So well thy words become thee as thy wounds;
They smack of honour both. – Go get him surgeons.

The major tragedies naturally provided many classic descriptions of injuries:

Queen. O, what a rash and bloody deed is this!

Hamlet, III, iv, 27

King. ... thy cicatrice[1] looks raw and red ...

Hamlet, IV, iii, 60

[281]

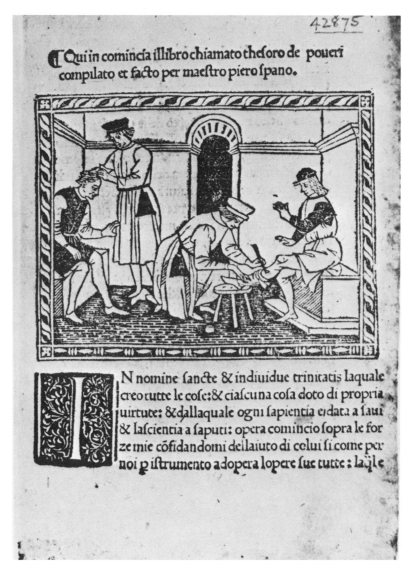

The interior of a Renaissance Hospital for poor patients, from
Thesaurus pauperum by Petrus Hispanus, 1497.
(Courtesy of the Wellcome Institute Library, London.)

Cornwall. . . . I bleed apace,[2]
Untimely comes this hurt. Give me your arm.

King Lear, III, vii, 96

Romeo and Juliet, more than any other play, has an excessive use of words with double and triple meanings; in this case there is a pun on the words 'grave man' with a double meaning (III, i, 91):

Mercutio, Go, villain, fetch a surgeon
Romeo, Courage, man; the hurt cannot be much.
Mercutio. No, 'tis not so deep as a well, nor so wide as a church door, but 'tis enough, 'twill serve. Ask for me tomorrow, and you shall find me a grave man.

The extent of the practice of surgery was described by Thomas Gale, the Royal Sergeant-Surgeon, in his book *Certain Workes of Chirurgerie, newly compiled and published* (1563), when he wrote:

... the chirurgion divideth continuitie, either by incision, by cutting off, the letting of blood, or by scarification. That which is divided he conjoyneth by adglutination of wounds, and by restoring of displaced bones into the place againe, and also by curing of fractures, that is to say broken bones. And he cutteth away superfluous matter by taking awaie tumours against nature ... as in extirpation divers waies of Ganglia, Cancer, and others of that kind. Either else in draining of water out of the bellie in Hidrops, or else in cutting off a superfluous finger ... or else taking awaie of Cataracts, or the web* in the eies. For trulie these be the chief duties of a Chirurgion, and the operations which he ought most trustilie to execute.

---

*'Eyes blind with the pin and web' (*Winter's Tale,* I, ii, 290).

ANNO·ÆTATIS.
68

Ambroise Paré (1510-1590) achieved fame as a surgeon on the battlefield, and then went on to develop new and improved techniques for dealing with wounds and controlling haemorrhage, and devised better surgical instruments. He was a master surgeon on his own merits, despite a lack of academic credentials. (Woodcut portrait, courtesy of the New York Academy of Medicine Library.)

Every surgeon today would echo the words of Lady Macbeth (I, v, 49): 'that my keen knife see not the wounds it makes.'

Caesar tells Antony (*Antony and Cleopatra*, V, i, 36): 'we do lance diseases in our bodies.'

In one short, bloody scene in *Othello*, Iago plans to get rid of both Roderigo and Cassio; he has induced Roderigo to ambush and attack Cassio. Cassio, however, wounds Roderigo and is unhurt until Iago slips behind and stabs him in the

A dentist at work. Dentistry was practised by
anyone who was brave enough to acquire the skills.
Many quacks posed as tooth-drawers and
displayed their technique in the street before
audiences of passers-by. Engraving by Lucas van
Leyden, 1523. (Courtesy of Rijksmuseum, Amsterdam.)

leg. Othello enters and, seeing Cassio wounded, concludes that Iago has killed him as arranged. In the darkened street, Iago stabs Roderigo to death. Realising that all this plotting is reaching a climax, Iago tries to get out of it, saying 'This is the night that either makes me or fordoes' me quite' (V, i, 129). In this chaotic mess we read (V, i, 71-94):

Iago. How is 't, brother?
Cassio. My leg is cut in two.
Iago. Marry, heaven forbid!
Light, gentlemen. I'll bind it with my shirt.
. . .
Who they should be that have thus mangled you?
. . .
These bloody accidents must excuse my manners.

Traumatic wounds were seldom allowed to heal by 'first intention', and fresh air was often considered detrimental to their healing:

Clifford. The air hath got into my deadly wounds,
And much effuse of blood doth make me faint.
                                    3 *King Henry VI*, II, vi, 27

Wounds were thus expected to heal slowly:

Iago. How poor are they that have not patience!
What wound did ever heal but by degrees?
                                    Othello, II, iii, 358

In *Antony and Cleopatra* (IV, vii, 6), we read:

Antony   ... Thou bleed'st apace.
Scarus. I had a wound here that was like a T,
But now 'tis made an H.

[286]

Surgery at the Salerno Medical School, near Naples: operations for
haemorrhoids, nasal polypi and cataract. This medical school had a
great influence throughout Europe. (From a 13th Century manuscript
in the British Library, London.)

Scarus probably refers to the benefits of enlarging a wound
from the shape of a T to an H in order to promote healing;
but he also puns on the letter 'H' and the word 'ache', which
was then often pronounced 'aitch'.

Wounds were dressed with ointments and salves, usually
vile, which would produce 'laudable pus'. This was considered an essential stage in the healing process. King Henry
VI refers to a wound 'being green' from laudable pus (2
King Henry VI, III, i, 285):

> Send succours, lords, and stop the rage betime,
> Before the wound do grow uncurable;
> For, being green, there is great hope of help.

[287]

The mortal danger of gangrene spurred barber-surgeons to act speedily and boldly; amputation – no other form of treatment would suffice. Menenius, a friend of the warrior Coriolanus, has this to say on amputation and gangrene (*Coriolanus*, III, i, 296):

> ... a limb that has but a disease
> Mortal, to cut it off: to cure it, easy.

And in the same scene (line 306) Sicinius says:

> The service of the foot,
> Being once gangren'd, is not then respected
> For what before it was.

A basic principle of surgery, that of removing a diseased member to save the rest of the body, is expressed by the Duke of York (*King Richard II*, V, iii, 85):

> This fest'red joint cut off, the rest rest sound;
> This let alone will all the rest confound.

Shakespeare, in his comments on wounds, makes many references to the use of the 'tent'. The 'tent' was a special roll of cloth or flax, which was stuffed into a wound to arrest bleeding and to absorb discharge during the healing process. When the 'tent' had absorbed as much discharge as it could, it tended to swell up and become smelly. Wounds were expected to suppurate, and 'laudable pus' was an essential stage in this process, while 'proud flesh' was the new tissue which grew from the depths of the wound till scar formation took place. Many references to the 'tent' occur in the more violent and tragic plays:

> *Marcus.* I have some wounds upon me, and they smart

An amputation, from *Feldtbuch der Wundartzney*
by Hans von Gersdorff, 1517.

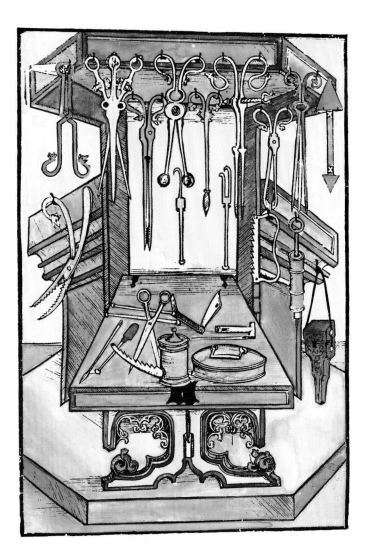

Surgical instruments of the Middle Ages; from
Hieronymus Brunschwig's *Chirugia*, 1497.
(Courtesy of the New York Academy of Medicine Library.)

Primitive crutches. Beggars and cripples relied on
folk-healers and were often left to their own resources.
(From *Topographica Hibernica* of Gerald of Wales.
MS. Roy, 13B, VIII, folio 30ᵛ, British Library, London.)

To hear themselves rememb'rd.
Cominius.   Should they not,
Well might they fester 'gainst ingratitude
And *tent* themselves with death.

Coriolanus, I, ix, 28

Cominius.   Go we to our *tent.*
The blood upon your visage dries; 'tis time
It should be look'd to.

Coriolanus, I, ix, 92

Menenius.   For 'tis a sore upon us
You cannot *tent* yourself . . .

Coriolanus, III, i, 235

Hector.　　　　　　　　The wound of peace is surety,
Surety secure; but modest doubt is call'd
The beacon of the wise, the *tent* that searches
To th' bottom of the worst.

Troilus and Cressida, II, ii, 14

Patroclus. Who keeps the *tent* now?
Thersites. The surgeon's box, or the patient's wound.

Troilus and Cressida, V, i, 10

Imogen. Talk thy tongue weary – speak.
I have heard I am a strumpet, and mine ear,
Therein false struck, can take no greater wound,
Nor *tent* to bottom that.

Cymbeline, III, iv, 111

Lear.　　　　　　　　Blasts and fogs upon thee!
Th' *untented* woundings of a father's curse
Pierce every sense about thee!

King Lear, I, iv, 299

Medical texts were traditionally written in Latin, and Dr Andrew Boorde (1490-1549), physician to King Henry VIII, was the first medical man to write a medical textbook in the English vernacular. In his *Breviary of Health* he spoke of surgeons with respect, but possibly expected higher standards than would would have been usual. He wrote:

> The Chirurgeon must have a goode eye and a stedfast hande (for chirurgy taketh its name of this). He must have goode witte and memory and goode judgement. Chirurgeons ought to be wyse and gentil, sober and circumspect. They muste be learned and not dronken. Nor must they promise more than they can perform with God's helpe.

A patient had to be brave and possibly fit to undergo

Theseus (Anthony Nicholls), Hippolyta (Stephanie Bidmead), Lysander
(Albert Finney), Hermia (Priscilla Morgan), Bottom (Charles Laughton),
Flute (Peter Woodthorpe), and Quince (Cyril Luckham), in Act V,
Scene I, of a production of *A Midsummer Night's Dream* by the
Shakespeare Memorial Theatre in 1959. Photograph by Angus McBean;
reproduced by courtesy of The Shakespeare Birthplace Trust.

surgery, and a surgeon even more so before undertaking it:

> *Pandulph.* Before the curing of a strong disease,
> Even in the instant of repair and health,
> The fit is strongest ...
>
> King John, III, iv, 112

Ellen Terry as Portia in *The Merchant of Venice* (Act IV, Scene I). From *The Complete Works of William Shakespeare* (c. 1910). Photograph: Window & Grove, London.

20
FAMILY
HISTORY

ILLIAM SHAKESPEARE'S father, John Shakespeare, was the son of a farmer from the village of Snitterfield, four miles north of Stratford-on-Avon, in Warwickshire. He left his fields to seek his fortune at Stratford, which was a commercial centre of some importance. Within a few years John Shakespeare had established himself as a glovemaker in Henley Street, with the right to place his stall on market days in a strategic location in the square, under the town clock. He went on to deal in woollens, leather, and various farm commodities, and as he prospered was appointed to a number of civic posts, including that of Chamberlain of the Common Council (the governing body of Stratford), alderman and bailiff. He was a successful man and had the good sense to make a marriage that would advance him socially.

Mary Arden, John Shakespeare's wife, was the daughter of Robert Arden, a man from whom John's father, Richard Shakespeare, rented his land. The Ardens belonged to the gentry, and claimed descent from the Ardens who had been 'Lords of Warrick' before the days of William the Conqueror. From the union of John Shakespeare and Mary

Arden, at least eight children were born. First came two girls, who died in infancy; then William was born in April, 1564. The exact day of his birth is not known, but tradition has accepted April 23, because this date made him exactly fifty-two years old at his death, which occurred on April 23, 1616. The record of the christening in the church register at Stratford is dated April 26. It would appear that the newborn infant was three days old when he was baptised, a customary age for a ceremony that was usually performed soon after birth in those days of high infant mortality.

William Shakespeare attended the Stratford Grammar School, a building which still stands today. In its low-ceilinged classrooms, furnished with oak desks and benches, the boys studied William Lilley's *Authorized Latin Grammar,* a textbook which was in general use in Renaissance England. William, according to his contemporary playwright Ben Jonson, 'learned little Latin and even less Greek'. What interested him was not only the world of books, but also the spectacle of life around him. Very little must have escaped his enquiring mind and powers of observation.

There is a period in Shakespeare's adolescence, from 1576 until 1582, for which few historical records are available; this probably corresponded to a decline in his father's fortunes. The glovemaker, experiencing financial difficulties, sold one of his wife's farms and mortgaged another property. He ceased attending meetings of the town council and gradually withdrew from public life. However, he was never poor or bankrupt, and the stories collected about his son's dropping out of school, his being apprenticed to a butcher and his poaching were probably all conjectures.

The threads are picked up again when William was eighteen years old. An entry in the register kept by the Bishop of Worcester revealed that a marriage licence was granted to William Shakespeare and Anne Hathaway in November, 1582. Anne was twenty-six years old, eight years his senior. She belonged to a family of well-to-do farmers who lived in a village named Shottery, about a mile from Stratford. Her house still stands today. It is a typical Tudor farmhouse, built of oak timber, with white-washed plaster walls, and a thick thatched roof between high brick chimneys.

At twenty-six Anne was, to say the least, an unusual match for William, who was virtually still a minor. When the marriage licence was issued, the bride was three months pregnant. A baby girl, Susanna, was born in the spring of the following year. The marriage, to judge by William's absences in London and possibly by his last will and testament, is sometimes considered to have been an unhappy one. He nicely points out the physiological moral of their disparity in ages in *Twelfth Night* (II, iv, 28):

> *Duke.* Too old, by heaven! Let still the woman take
> An elder than herself; so wear she to him,
> So sways she level in her husband's heart.
> For, boy, however we do praise ourselves,
> Our fancies are more giddy and unfirm,
> More longing, wavering, sooner lost and won,
> Then women's are.

A couple of years after the birth of Susanna, twins, a boy and a girl, were born; they were christened Hamnet and Judith, in honour of the Shakespeares' friends Hamnet and Judith Sadler, who lived on High Street. The children were very young when their father left in 1587 or 1588 to work in

London as an actor, leaving his wife and children behind.

William took a risk in trying to become an actor without a period of apprenticeship. He must have been driven by tremendous inward conviction as he sought out the field where his talents could receive full expression. Actors' wives usually followed or accompanied their husbands, but Anne did not, choosing to remain in Stratford. Shakespeare lived in rented lodgings and, strangely, maintained virtually no family ties.

At this period, there were four permanent theatres in London. No one knows with whom Shakespeare spent his early years as an actor. His connection with James Burbage and his two sons, Richard and Cuthbert, all actors and part owners of one of the theatres, was an early one, and it continued throughout his stage career.

As both actor and author, Shakespeare combined two talents that normally opposed each other. By 1592, at the age of twenty-eight years, he was sufficiently well known to arouse interest in his dual role of poet and actor, an unusual and extraordinary combination.

In this same year, 1592, the London theatres were closed because of the plague. The disease frequently broke out in the crowded city, known for its filthy streets and open drains; but this epidemic was so serious that all the theatres and places of entertainment were closed for two years. The acting companies, to keep themselves employed, went off on provincial tours, and the market for new plays dried up considerably. During this period Shakespeare wrote his two most famous poems on classical subjects, *Venus and Adonis* and *The Rape of Lucrece*.

William Shakespeare;
portrait by Gerard Soest (d. 1681).
From The Shakespeare Birthplace Trust,
Shakespeare Centre Library.

Above: Holy Trinity Church, Stratford-upon-Avon, where Shakespeare is buried. From The Shakespeare Birthplace Trust, Shakespeare Centre Library.

Right: Elizabeth Knott Garden, Stratford-upon-Avon. From The Shakespeare Birthplace Trust, Shakespeare Centre Library.

Anne Hathaway's cottage, Stratford-upon-Avon.
From The Shakespeare Birthplace Trust, Shakespeare Centre Library.

Hall's Croft, Stratford-upon-Avon.
From The Shakespeare Birthplace Trust, Shakespeare Centre Library.

The theatres reopened in June, 1594, after the epidemic had run its course, and some time that summer Shakespeare apparently joined a theatrical company called the Chamberlain's Men. We know from carefully kept Royal records that in December, when the Chamberlain's Men gave performances at Court, one of the players was William Shakespeare. We do not know whether Shakespeare was a good actor – there was probably no accepted means of judging; the leading parts in many plays were taken by Richard Burbage, who acted the roles of Hamlet, Richard III, King Lear and Othello. Apparently Shakespeare was quite content with minor parts, like that of the ghost in *Hamlet*, which was one of his standbys.

His profession proved sufficiently profitable to enable him to purchase a house. This he did in 1597 at Stratford, and called it the New Place. It was one of the largest houses in Stratford, and had been built about one hundred years earlier. He had it renovated, and New Place became one of the best-known properties in the neighbourhood.

After the death of Queen Elizabeth I, King James arrived in London in 1603. He took over the Chamberlain's Men and gave the company permission to take the name of the King's Men. By then they had a new theatre, the Globe, which was considered the best in London. Shakespeare was one of the shareholders.

He returned to Stratford and retired to New Place in 1611, when he was still young and at the summit of fame and fortune. His parents had died. Susanna, his eldest daughter, had married in 1607 the physician Dr John Hall. In February, 1616, the remaining twin, Judith, married Thomas

[297]

Quiney, a merchant and the son of a close family friend. Two months after her marriage Shakespeare died – on April 23, 1616. No one knows the cause of his death for certain. In his will, written on March 25, he declared himself to be in a perfect state of 'health and memorie'. He left his property to his descendants and made small bequests to various friends and relatives. His second-best bed was left to his wife! Possibly it was the bed the couple had slept in, the best bed in the house being reserved for visitors.

Having been a lay rector of the Church of the Holy Trinity, Shakespeare was privileged to be buried inside the church. Over his grave are inscribed the lines:

> Good friend, for Jesus' sake forbear
> To dig the dust enclosed here.
> Blessed be the man that spares these stones
> And cursed be he that moves my bones.

The threat conveyed in these lines has probably helped to maintain his bones undisturbed in a crowded burial ground for three and a half centuries. He still rests there today, in the silence of the beautiful chancel of the Holy Trinity Church. It has become a place of pilgrimage, and has been visited by countless millions from every corner of the globe.

BIBLIOGRAPHY

ABT, I.A., & GARRISON, F.H. *History of Pediatrics*, Saunders, Philadelphia, 1965.

BONSER, W. *The Medical Background of Anglo-Saxon England*, Wellcome Hist. Med. Lib., London, 1963.

BROWN, I.J.C. *How Shakespeare Spent the Day*, Bodley Head, London, 1963.

BROWN, I.J.C. *Shakespeare in his Time*, Nelson, Edinburgh, 1960.

BUCKNILL, J.C. *The Medical Knowledge of Shakespeare*, Longmans, London, 1860.

BUCKNILL, J.C. *The Mad Folk of Shakespeare*, Macmillan, London, 1867.

CASTIGLIONI, A. *A History of Medicine*, Knopf, New York, 1941.

CHANDLER, S.B. Shakespeare and Sleep, *Bull. Hist. Med.*, 1955, 29:255.

COPEMAN, W.S.C. *Doctors and Disease in Tudor Times*, Dawson, London, 1960.

CUTTER, I.S., & VIETS, H.R. *A Short History of Midwifery*, Saunders, Philadelphia, 1964.

DAVISON, A. Shakespeare: Some Medical Problems, *Scot. Soc. Hist. Med., Rep. Proc.*, 1963-64, 14.

DRAPER, J.W. The Humors – Some Psychological Aspects of Shakespeare's Tragedies, *J. Amer. med. Ass.*, 1964, 188:259.

EDITORIAL. The Doctor in Shakespeare, *Canad. med. Ass. J.*, 1964, 90:792.

FORBES, T.R. *The Midwife and the Witch*, Yale Univ. Press, 1966.

GANDEVIA, B. Shakespeare and Chaucer: Their Use of Medical Allusion in the Story of Troilus and Criseyde, *R. Melb. Hosp. clin. Rep.*, 1953, 23:72.

GETCHELL, A.C. The Medical Knowledge of Shakespeare, *Boston med. surg. J.*, 1907, 156: 65, 109.

GRAHAM, H. *Eternal Eve – The Mysteries of Birth and the Customs that Surround It*, Hutchinson, London, 1960.

GREEN-ARMYTAGE, V.B. Gynaecology and Obstetrics in Shakespeare, *J. Obstet. Gynaec. Brit. Cwlth*, 1930, 37:272.

JAMES, T. Madness in Shakespeare, *S. Afr. med. J.*, 1961, 35:154.

MARTIN, W.S. Shakespeare, Medicine and the Law, *Canad. med. Ass. J.*, 1965, 93:255.

McGEOCH, A.H. Shakespeare the Dermatologist, *Aust. J. Derm.*, 1955, 3:53.

McGEOCH, A.H. Shakespeare the Syphilologist, *Med. J. Aust.*, 1960, 1:348.

McKENZIE, D. *The Infancy of Medicine*, Macmillan, London, 1927.

NOVA ET VETERA. Shakespeare's 'Insane Root', *Brit. med. J.*, 1907, 1:290.

PARTRIDGE, E. *Shakespeare's Bawdy*, Routledge & Kegan Paul, London, 1968.

PHAIRE, T. *The Boke of Chyldren*, reprinted by Livingstone, Edinburgh, 1965.

ROGERS, L. W. *The Ghosts in Shakespeare*, Theo Book Co., New York, 1972.

ROWSE, A. L. *Sex and Society in Shakespeare's Age*, Scribner, New York, 1974.

RYDÉN, M. *Shakespearean Plant Names: Identifications and Interpretations*, Almqvist & Wiksell, Stockholm, 1978. (*Acta Univ. Stockh.* Stockholm Studies in English: 43.)

SIMPSON, R.R. *Shakespeare and Medicine*, Livingstone, Edinburgh, 1959.

TEMKIN, O. *The Falling Sickness*, Johns Hopkins Press, Baltimore, 1971.

THOMPSON, C.J.S. *The Mystic Mandrake*, University Books, New York.

WHEELWRIGHT, E. G. *The Physick Garden*, Jonathan Cape, London, 1939.

WILLIAMS, P. *Life in Tudor England*, Batsford, Putnam, 1964.

WILSON, F. P. *The Plague in Shakespeare's London*, Oxford Univ. Press, 1927.

WILSON, J. D. *What Happens in Hamlet*, Cambridge Univ. Press, 1970.

GLOSSARY

CHAPTER 1

[1]outward worth: visible wealth
[2]simples operative: medicinal herbs
[3]child-changed: affected by the behaviour of his children
[4]sway: direction
[5]temperance: sanity
[6]even o'er: go over
[7]stay his cure: delay his cure
[8]convinces ... art: defeats the efforts of medical science
[9]presently amend: immediately recover
[10]annoyance: harm
[11]still: continuously
[12]mated: amazed
[13]movers: causes
[14]cunning: skill
[15]turning o'er: studying
[16]infusions: distillates used for treatment
[17]vegetives: plants
[18]mortality: the fact that all men must die
[19]congregated college: the whole Royal College of Physicians
[20]inaidable estate: incurable condition
[21]empirics: quacks
[22]tinct and multiplying med'cine: the nature and medicinal value of gold
[23]more science: expert knowledge
[24]formal: normal
[25]mortified: dead
[26]presecuted ... hope: kept on pestering time with the vain hope of cure

CHAPTER 2

[1]barr'd: prevented
[2]between ... dream: the interval between the first idea and the dreadful deed itself is like a hideous apparition or a nightmare
[3]genius ... insurrection: the mind ('genius') and the body ('mortal instruments'), and a man's whole nature, are like a kingdom in a state of war
[4]formal: normal
[5]frenzy: madness
[6]holp: helped
[7]medicinal: healing
[8]humour: mental illness
[9]mole: blemish
[10]pales: defences
[11]o'erleavens: mixes with
[12]plausive: agreeable
[13]nature's livery: i.e., inborn
[14]fortune's star: the result of ill luck

CHAPTER 3

[1]humour: whim
[2]frame: design
[3]my ... bedlam: I must now pretend to be a melancholic and sigh like a lunatic beggar. Tom o'Bedlam was a lunatic discharged from Bedlam
[4]proof ... precedent: examples
[5]mortified: numbed
[6]low: humble
[7]pelting: paltry
[8]bans: curses
[9]gate: i.e., brain
[10]times' plague: a sign of these diseased times
[11]free: i.e., from cares
[12]when ... fellowship: when we see better men than ourselves suffering, our own sufferings seem slight. A man who suffers endures most in his mind, because he contrasts his present misery with his happy past; but when he has companions in misery ('bearing fellowship') his mind suffers less.
[13]antic disposition: mad behaviour
[14]fruitful river: stream of tears
[15]dejected ... visage: downcast countenance

[16]play: act, as in a play
[17]trappings: ornaments
[18]canon: rule, law
[19]outrageous: cruel
[20]sea: i.e., an endless turmoil
[21]by opposing: i.e., committing suicide
[22]consummation: completion
[23]fardels: burdens, such as a labourer's pack
[24]bourn: boundary
[25]will: ability to act
[26]salt: bawdy
[27]season: make ready; literally, salt
[28]tubs and baths: treatment of syphilis by hot baths
[29]spital-house: hospital for venereal disease
[30]cast the gorge: vomit
[31]fell: fearful
[32]general filths: common harlots
[33]hold fast: don't pay your debts
[34]bound servants: apprentices, bound by an agreement to serve faithfully
[35]pill: rob (pillage)
[36]lin'd: padded
[37]domestic awe: obedience due to parents
[38]neighbourhood: neighbourliness
[39]mysteries: skilled trades, in which the spirit of brotherhood is strong
[40]decline: fall away
[41]confounding contraries: destructive opposites
[42]halt: limp
[43]liberty: licentiousness
[44]blains: sores
[45]merely: entirely

CHAPTER 4

[1]Neapolitan bone-ache: bony pain from the Neapolitan disease or syphilis
[2]placket: opening in a petticoat or skirt; i.e., a wench
[3]in Naples: a reference to the Neapolitan disease
[4]speak i' the nose: the nasal bones damaged by syphilis, a late manifestation
[5]French ... all: loss of hair from the French disease
[6]shaved: caught venereal disease
[7]jollity: a reference to the losing of hair from venereal disease

[8]spital: hospital

[9]galled: sore

[10]goose of Winchester: prostitutes were called Winchester geese because they inhabited property in Southwark owned by the Bishop of Winchester

[11]figuring: imagining

[12]of ... o'er: may every disease suffered by man or beast cover you all over with blotches

[13]brutish sting: lust

[14]embossed sores .. foot: carbuncles and boils that result from licentious living; i.e., skin manifestation of syphilis

[15]spital-house: hospital for venereal diseases

[16]cast the gorge: vomit

[17]spital: hospital

[18]powd'ring tub: tub used for the treatment of venereal disease

[19]lazar kite: beggar

[20]Cressid's kind: Cressida, the pattern of loose women, ended her days in the hospital for venereal diseases.

[21]salt: bawdy

[22]season: make ready; literally, salt

[23]tubs and baths: the treatment of venereal disease by hot tub baths

[24]tub-fast: the sweating treatment

[25]mar ... spurring: because of sore heels

[26]quillets: subtleties

[27]hoar: cover with white blotches

[28]flamen: priest

[29]quality: nature

[30]down with the nose

[31]his particular ... general weal: a difficult phrase; the general meaning is 'he that in following his own desires separates himself from the general good'

[32]unscarr'd braggarts: unwounded boasters

CHAPTER 5

[1]falling sickness: epilepsy

[2]ope his doublet: open his short coat

[3]lethargy: illness, i.e., epilepsy

[4]casing: enclosing

[5]cribb'd: hampered

[6]saucy: insolent

[7]upon a thought: as quick as a thought
[8]extend his passion: increase his fit
[9]straight: straight away
[10]wrought the mure: worn the wall thin
[11]speak lower: quietly
[12]dull and favourable: drowsy and kindly
[13]changes: i.e., changes colour

CHAPTER 6

[1]prodigious: unnatural
[2]child-bed privilege: the privilege of lying-in after confinement
[3]'longs: belongs
[4]seedness: sowing; in this case, conception
[5]foison: plenty
[6]moulded: conceived
[7]good ... her: may she have an easy pregnancy
[8]great-bellied women: in the last stages of pregnancy
[9]rams: battering rams
[10]shake the press: charge the crowd
[11]saving ... reverence: begging your honour's pardon
[12]legs forward: a reference to presentation with extended legs
[13]curtail'd: cut short
[14]proportion: shape
[15]dissembling: cheating
[16]halt: limp
[17]increase: childbearing
[18]derogate: debased
[19]teem: conceive
[20]spleen: malice
[21]thwart disnatur'd: perverse and unnatural
[22]cadent: falling
[23]fret: wear away
[24]prodigy: monster
[25]enfranchised: set free, delivered
[26]law: i.e., of nature
[27]untimely ripp'd: taken from his mother's womb after her death
[28]mettle: material
[29]something: somewhat
[30]took ... death: swore solemnly, as he was on his deathbed
[31]dividant: divided

CHAPTER 7

[1]come to any proof: stand the test
[2]greensickness: a kind of anaemia, like anorexia nervosa, seen in young unmarried women
[3]get: beget
[4]inflammation: the heating effects of alcohol
[5]sherris-sack: a Spanish wine, sherry
[6]crudy: crude
[8]forgetive: quick to invent
[8]liver: regarded as the seat of the passions, especially of courage
[9]commences: gives it its degree
[10]husbanded: cultivated
[11]monstrous: unnatural
[12]wash my brain: by drinking
[13]pleasance: have a gay time
[14]warder: guardian
[15]limbec: a still
[16]clepe: call
[17]swinish: gross
[18]soil our addition: smirch our honour
[19]fustian: nonsense; literally, cheap cloth
[20]poop: stern
[21]bubukles: large boils – a word coined by Fluellen from 'bubo' and 'carbuncles'
[22]whelks: pimples
[23]courtesy: politeness

CHAPTER 8

[1]husbandry: agriculture
[2]leas: open lands
[3]coulter: blade of the plowshoe
[4]deracinate: uproot
[5]mead: meadow
[6]burnet: a weed with a brown flower
[7]docks ... kecksies: weeds that grow in neglected meadows
[8]secure hour: time of relaxation
[9]porches: entrance
[10]posset: curdle
[11]eager: acid

¹²sustaining: which maintains life

¹³corse: corpse

¹⁴seeming and savour: appearance and fragrance

¹⁵gear: stuff

¹⁶trunk: body

¹⁷maw: stomach

CHAPTER 9

¹rose: the Red Rose of the House of Lancaster

²sanguine: cowardly

³sanguine star: red birthmark

⁴purge this choler: blood-letting, a recognized treatment for certain illnesses; choler, excess of bile, anger

⁵conclude: come to terms

⁶put ... purgation: give him treatment by purgatives

⁷blue eye and sunken: with dark rings under the eye

⁸unquestionable: glum

⁹having ... revenue: your beard anyhow is a poor thing, like the income of a
younger brother

¹⁰bonnet unbanded: hat without a band

¹¹bourn: boundary

¹²will: resolution, ability to act

CHAPTER 10

¹sands: the sands in an hour-glass

²incident: accompanying

³swain: rustic

⁴carve ... point: carve out a sundial on the grass

⁵ean: bring forth young

⁶homely curds: simple food made of milk curd

⁷secure: without a care

⁸delicates: delicacies

⁹curious: elaborate

¹⁰mewling: whimpering

¹¹ballad: poem

¹²pard: leopard

¹³jealous in honour: sensitive about his humour

¹⁴bubble reputation: fame quickly burst as a bubble

[15]good capon lin'd: bribed with the present of a fat chicken. It was common knowledge that those who wished for justice from a county magistrate had to bring presents with them. Such magistrates were known as 'basket justices'.

[16]formal cut: severe pattern

[17]saws: sayings

[18]modern instances: commonplace illustrations

[19]pantaloon: the foolish old man of comedy

CHAPTER 11

[1]alt'ring rheums: diseases which change his nature

[2]unbashful forehead: vicious boldness

[3]means of: the pleasures that bring

[4]confine: boundary, edge

[5]hams: knee joints

[6]way of life: the correct reading, according to Dr Johnson, is 'May' (i.e., springtime), as the use of the word 'May' for youth at its prime is common

[7]sear, sere: dried up and withered

[8]stigmatical in making: deformed in body

[9]long ingrafted condition: temper which has long been part of his nature

[10]take ... top: take time by the forelock; i.e., make the most of the present

[11]bestow: place

[12]crazy: decrepit

[13]heyday: excitement

[14]grained: lined

[15]lamps: eyes

CHAPTER 12

[1]mortality: life

[2]invisible: without any outward signs

[3]death ... mind: death, having attacked the visible parts of the body, now leaves them and strikes inward; i.e., there are now no outward symptoms of a sickness, but his brain is affected

[4]which ... themselves: his delirious ravings, crowding in upon his mind, which is the last stronghold of life, contradict themselves

[5]cygnet: young swan, heir

[6]chants ... death: it was a popular belief that swans sang only once, just before their death

[7]organ pipe of frailty: frail mortal voice

[8]it ... doors: I could not die indoors

[9]glass ... run: reference to sands of time in an hour-glass

[10]timely-parted: died naturally

[11]being all descended: because all the blood has descended

[12]lodged: laid flat

[13]posset: curdle

[14]eager: acid

[15]still: always

[16]grace: power of goodness

[17]rude will: natural desire for soil

[18]dangerous conceits: dangerous thoughts

[19]embassage: messenger

[20]taper: life's candle

[21]darkness: death

[22]butt: aim

[23]sea-mark: a conspicuous object by which a sailor checks his course

[24]and ... sail: the mark that I have reached the end of my voyage, i.e., the end of life

[25]sea: i.e., an endless turmoil

[26]consummation: completion

[27]rub: impediment

[28]shuffled ... coil: cast off the fuss of life

[29]makes ... life: makes it a calamity to have so long a life

[30]contumely: insulting behaviour

[31]insolence of office: insolent behaviour of government officials

[32]spurns ... takes: insults which men of merit have patiently to endure from the unworthy

[33]quietus: discharge

[34]bodkin: dagger

[35]fardels: burdens, the labourer's pack

[36]bourn: boundary

[37]will: ability to act, resolution

[38]resolution: ability to act

[39]cast: colour

[40]pitch: height, used in the swarming flight of hawks

[41]with ... action: by the brooding on this thought, great enterprises are diverted from their course and fade away

CHAPTER 13

¹pretty: a pretty notion
²atomies: smallest particles
³advance: raise
⁴deficient ... headlong: my sight failing, cause me to topple headlong
⁵counterfeit'st: imitates
⁶bark: boat
⁷mote: speck of dust
⁸sense: sight, eyes
⁹sans: without
¹⁰mope: be dull
¹¹tinct: colour
¹²savour: stink

CHAPTER 14

¹cranks: winding passages, or, in this case, blood-vessels
²offices: parts of the house (or body) where work is done
³nerves: sinews
⁴me: the liver
⁵vents: utters
⁶mangled forms: quaint phrases
⁷tackle: rigging
⁸shrouds: sails
⁹stay: hold
¹⁰empty all these veins: blood-letting
¹¹spirits: vital energy
¹²wills: desires

CHAPTER 15

¹owed: owned
²moe: more
³cast: inspect
⁴pristine: former
⁵mummers: dancers in miming dances in which they disguised themselves
⁶set ... against: declared war upon, a red flag being a sign of defiance
⁷bleeding: unheeded; also reference to bloody motions
⁸bate: grow thin
⁹holp: helped
¹⁰map of woe: picture of sorrow

[11]water: diagnosis by inspection of the urine
[12]owed: owned or possessed
[13]smack: taste
[14]saltness: probably the 'saltness of age' as contrasted with the 'freshness of youth'
[15]Galen: the Greek physician, who was still much studied in Shakespeare's time
[16]by the heels: by putting you in stocks
[17]gall: irritate
[18]vaward: vanguard
[19]wags: high-spirited lads
[20]characters: signs
[21]single: feeble
[22]degrees: youth and age
[23]prevent: forestall; i.e., both youth and age have their own curses already
[24]commodity: advantage
[25]scann'd: examined

CHAPTER 16

[1]rankle: make fester
[2]death tokens, token'd pestilence: plague spots; the reddish petechial rash which indicates a fatal turn

CHAPTER 17

[1]incident: accompanying
[2]distempered: sick, but not fatally
[3]broken: with the skin broken
[4]sovereign'st: most excellent
[5]parmaceti: spermaceti, a fatty substance found in whales and used as an ointment
[6]med'cine potable: gold in solution, called 'aurum potable' and regarded as a medicine of great worth
[7]unintelligent of our insufficience: not able to realise one's shortcomings
[8]possets: warm drink of milk and ale, taken as a nightcap
[9]stomach-qualm'd: have a feeling of nausea
[10]devouring pestilence: consuming illness
[11]sable-coloured: black
[12]black oppressing humour: melancholy
[13]empirics: quacks

[14]stay his cure: wait for time to heal them
[15]convinces ... art: reflects the attempts of the medical art
[16]presently: immediately
[17]swoln and ulcerous: i.e., tuberculous lymph glands
[18]discharg'd: gone from him
[19]cease: suspend
[20]hent: leap

CHAPTER 18

[1]fondling: caressing
[2]pale: fence
[3]bottom grass: grass growing in a damp valley
[4]brakes: bushes
[5]rouse: disturb – a hunting term
[6]pike: presumably penis
[7]muddy conger: conger eel
[8]blow down: deflowered
[9]marry: by the Virgin Mary, an oath
[10]rational: reasonable
[11]got: begotten
[12]metal: material
[13]country matters: something indecent
[14]dug: nipple
[15]button: i.e., at the top
[16]bauble: penis
[17]tale: an erotic pun on penis
[18]graff: graft
[19]horn-mad: like a mad bull; Adriana thinks her husband is accusing her of infidelity
[20]security: carelessness
[21]presently: immediately
[22]horning: cuckolding
[23]doubted: suspected
[24]singled: separated
[25]mart: market
[26]sodden: rotten
[27]raw ... entertainment: show lack of experience in entertaining her customers
[28]difference of all complexions: men of every land

²⁹prescript: prescribed
³⁰strossers: underpants
³¹jade: old worn-out horse
³²leecher: copulate
³³luxury: lust
³⁴minces virtue: walks with a great air of virtue
³⁵fitchew: polecat
³⁶soiled horse: fed on spring grass
³⁷centaurs: creatures half man and half animal
³⁸mountant: uplifted
³⁹let ... smoke: let the heat of your lust overcome the smoke of his eloquence
⁴⁰yet ... contrary: may you in your turn suffer from venereal disease for six months
⁴¹thatch ... dead: curly golden hair is often borrowed, its owner being a corpse!
⁴²pox of wrinkles: to hell with wrinkles – because paint will conceal them
⁴³rheum: moisture
⁴⁴carbuncles: means also boils
⁴⁵declining ... aspect: looking downward
⁴⁶armadoes of caracks: fleets of big merchant ships
⁴⁷ballast: laden

CHAPTER 19

¹cicatrice: scar
²apace: rapidly
³fordoes: ruins

INDEX